W H  C I T Y

THE POETRY OF DUNDEE AND ITS HINTERLAND

WHALEBACK CITY

THE POETRY OF DUNDEE AND ITS HINTERLAND
EDITED BY W.N. HERBERT AND ANDY JACKSON

Dundee

First published in Great Britain in 2013
by Dundee University Press
University of Dundee, DD1 4HN
www.dundee.ac.uk/dup

Copyright © W.N. Herbert & Andy Jackson 2013

ISBN: 9781845861445

British Library Cataloguing-in-Publication Data
A catalogue record for this book is available on request from the
British Library

Designed and Typeset by Freight Design (Scotland) Ltd.

Printed and Bound in Great Britain by
Bell & Bain Ltd, Glasgow

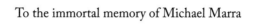

To the immortal memory of Michael Marra

WITH THANKS

A project like this could never work without the advice and assistance of others, so the editors are indebted to the following for their contribution to this book;

Great thanks go to Michael Bolik and the Archives staff at the University of Dundee for helping us to unearth many lost poetic treasures. Thanks also to Professor David Robb from the School of English for his advice and support.

Thanks also to Lizzie MacGregor and the staff at the Scottish Poetry Library for helping to track down poems and their authors. The SPL is a genuine national treasure.

Thanks to Ross Stewart and Ryan Rushton for their legwork on behalf of Dundee University Press, and to Anna Day for her faith in the project and for carrying it through.

Thanks also go to the Marra family for their generosity in letting us use Michael's wonderful words at the saddest time imaginable. Thanks also to Anne Holton for the wonderful afternoon we spent going over Harvey Holton's poetic legacy – we are proud to be able to bring some of his poems to press for the first time, and hopefully his collected poems will follow some day. We would also like to thank Clara Young for helping to supply the poetry of her late father Douglas, and Matthew Fitt for championing another 'lost' Dundee poet in William Beharrie.

Huge respect is due also to Andrew Murray Scott for his particularly helpful support and advice, and also for being the glue that has held Dundee's literary scene together across four decades.

Many thanks are due to the editors and publishers who allowed us to reproduce previously-published poems in this anthology. Thanks also to the poets themselves, many of whom provided advice and gave their poems and their time so freely; Kate Armstrong, Donald Campbell, Robert Crawford, Pippa Little, Ellie MacDonald, Carl MacDougall, Sean O'Brien, Lydia Robb, Stan Smith, Anne Stevenson, Jim Stewart and Richard Watt.and to all the others who took time to respond.

INTRODUCTION

'Due west, Balgay rises
whalebacked from a
sea of suburban grey'.
(James Adams)

Dundee is one of those places that people apart from its own citizens have only a vague relationship with, but that its sons and daughters obsess over with all the passion of the neglected. It is, like its football teams, in the second rank of Scottish cities, leaving Edinburgh and Glasgow to fight for primacy in political, economic, and, usually, cultural terms.

It never commits the folly of imagining, as metropolises often do, that it could stand for the nation, or even be a substitute for it, fronting up for Scotland to the world. Its temptation is rather that of withdrawal, of introversion, picking over local history and its minor figures with the meticulousness of the collector.

Nonetheless, it is a city that, every now and then, punches well above its weight in literary terms. Now is one of those times, in which it has nurtured a host of poets and novelists, mostly born in the fifties and sixties, thus catching the last benefits of the Welfare State before Thatcher closed the door on society. Their imaginations mostly came into fruit between two anagrammatic dates: the Devolution debacle of 1979 and the limited freedoms offered by the referendum for the Scottish Parliament in 1997.

Dundee's leet of literati includes Bill Duncan, John Glenday, Tracey Herd, A.L. Kennedy, James Meek, Don Paterson and many more – it's a substantial haul for a town which has spent the last thirty years in industrial decline with a falling population – indeed a number of these writers too have chosen to leave to work elsewhere. In the same period, a significant influx of visiting writers have invigorated the city to differing degrees, some settling nearby or, rather, nearby St Andrews, including Colette Bryce, John Burnside, Douglas Dunn, Kirsty Gunn, Kathleen Jamie, Sean O'Brien, and Val Warner.

Historically, too, there are three or four moments where Dundee's cultural role does briefly become that of microcosm for the nation, where what is happening in Dundee either mirrors or anticipates what is happening in Scotland.

The first is a street brawl, a stabbing in the city centre, which just happens to have enormous political consequences, and therefore finds its way into a poem. The victim was, according to legend, the arrogant son of the English constable, Selby, and the murderer a teenage William Wallace. The poet, brutal and witty by turns, was the late fifteenth century bard, Blind Harry, author of *The Wallace*.

Fleeing the scene, Wallace is saved by the quick-wittedness of a local woman, who disguises him in 'A roussat goun of hir awn', and he sets to spinning: *'In that same hous thai socht him beselye/Bot he sat still and span full conandly...'* Prefigured in this rapid alternation between naked aggression and cross-dressed cunning, between the edge of the male dagger and the sharp thinking of the 'gud wiff', is much of the character of subsequent Dundonian writing.

The next key moment is in the mid-sixteenth century, when Dundee is a hotbed of Protestant thought – not yet the Calvinism which will, under John Knox and his successors, cast such a distinctive pall over the Scottish mind, but the radical Lutheranism of the likes of George Wishart, martyred in St Andrews in 1546.

Dundee, as a significant East Coast port, was a point of importation for ideas as well as claret. This had its most distinct intellectual impact on the minds of three brothers, James, John and Robert Wedderburn, who between them produced work in poetry, prose and drama: a complete literary oeuvre in Scots, in the incomplete remnants of which we find the new ideas argued out across religious and political lines.

The eldest brother, James, is supposed to have written two poetic dramas which were performed in Dundee, satires on the Church which have not survived, before fleeing to France in 1540. The youngest, Robert, who inherited the family sinecure of Vicar of Dundee, composed the Scots prose work *The Complaynt of Scotlande* in 1549, a rallying call for unity in the face of the Rough Wooing.

Their brother, John, is reckoned to have had the major part in the composition around 1547 of *The Gude and Godlie Ballates*, a distinctive combination of Protestant doctrinal poems and purified versions of secular ballads, before he too had to go into exile.

However, most Dundonians who care to look for Dundee's place in the poetry world may well start on the internet rather than the sixteenth century, stumbling instead upon *poetryatlas.com*, a worthy online project attempting to gather poems of place into one searchable world map.

Hovering their expectant mouse over the Dundee area, they would find a dozen poems referencing Baldovan, Broughty Ferry, Mains Castle – oh, yes, and that bridge across the silvery Tay. Looking closer, they would find that every single poem listed on *poetryatlas.com* is by William Topaz McGonagall. In fact, ask most Scots to name a Dundonian poet and it's a pound to a peh they'll say McGonagall.

The fascination with MacGonagall extends so far beyond that audience which can be presumed to have an interest in poetry, let alone what was thought to be poetry in a small Northern European country in the late nineteenth century, that it becomes a different category of phenomenon.

One key element of this continuing interest is undoubtedly satiric: a critique of poetry as it is conceived of by those who don't really want to read it. According to this take, MacGonagall, a rude mechanical, wrote laughably bad poems which betrayed his pretensions to be something better than he was – and so, think the thoughtless, do all poets.

What this viewpoint does is place his work beyond literary judgement and into a purely sociological context. MacGonagall is funny, but hardly extra-literary: bad poetry is poetry too, and Dundee is diverse enough to contain both him, the Wedderburns and William Wallace – plus further quantities of the good stuff over the last one hundred years.

MacGonagall's magnificent manglings were followed by the Scottish Renaissance with its revival of nationalist culture – in particular, the return to the rich extended vocabulary of literary Scots. Broughty Ferry-born Lewis Spence was an early pioneer in this field. Dundee's war poet Joseph Lee, as well as recording life in the trenches, inspired other servicemen of the Great War to write about the Great War. William Montgomery, who engaged with the New Apocalyptics movement of the 1940s and early 50s, and was still publishing into the 1980s, provides a bridge between the first half of the 20th Century and the writing of recent decades.

In the 1970s and 1980s the city saw an explosion of interest in poetry and literature, with a number of small presses turning out influential magazines such as *AMF*, *Gallimaufry* and *Gairfish*, and also the two landmark anthologies *Seagate* and *Seagate II*. Writers in Scots began to claim back the language of the city and the suburbs in the 1980s and 1990s – Kate Armstrong, Matthew Fitt, Harvey Holton, Ellie MacDonald and others. In a pivotal 1994 episode of The South Bank Show exploring the new generation of UK poets, no less than five of the twenty featured poets were based within thirty miles of Dundee.

In between these movements in Dundee-based literature are a few singular, and singularly unplaceable, characters – Syd Scroggie, blind hillwalker, and Mary Brooksbank, chronicler of working-class life in the mills and foundries of the city, whose legacy might be most evident in the work of the 'Tribal Tongues' poetry of contemporary figures Gary Robertson and Mark Thomson. We also nod here to that generation of poets who are part of the current literary framework in and around the city – Dawn Wood, Judith Taylor and others.

In any representation of the literature of a small city, there is always a tension between literary standards and representation, between exclusivity on aesthetic terms, and inclusivity on societal ones. 'X may not be in the first rank,' one side of this argument might go, 'but he or she is representative.' The editors have instead selected that aspect of the work of excellent writers which focuses on Dundee; and the most successful work by those writers who may, in the compendious scheme of Scottish literature, be regarded as representatives for the city.

This volume is dedicated to a writer at once completely Dundonian, and unquestionably among the greats: Michael Marra. Debate may continue as to whether he was the closest Scotland came to its own Bob Dylan or to its own Tom Waits, but we believe, in its directness, freedom from pretension, and the vibrant use of Dundonian, his work is a perfect ambassador for the Dundonian character.

Whaleback City celebrates the richness and depth of poetry rooted in and around Dundee, stretching back over five centuries. Its poems touch on many aspects of the city – what it is to be Dundonian, as well as what it means to visit or live in the city as an incomer. Some poems are love poems to the city, its people or its environs, while others portray Dundee's less celebrated past. Some poems describe the majesty of the Tay, while others praise that same river for conveying them quickly past. These poems tell of the city in the full and complex range of its moods and guises.

In all our choices, we have been mindful of the duty of poetry to re-present the world to us, to challenge our perceptions rather than confirm our convictions. We hope you find the result as illuminating as it is illustrative of a town that once was radical in religious terms, and for many years defined itself as radical politically, and has now become a radical new centre of Scottish poetry.

W.N. Herbert & Andy Jackson
June 2013

CONTENTS

THE TAY

THE TOWN

THE TEMPER

1
THE TAY

TAY BRIDGE
Douglas Dunn

A sky that tastes of rain that's still to fall
And then of rain that falls and tastes of sky ...
The colour of the country's moist and subtle
In dusk's expected rumour. Amplify
All you can see this evening and the broad
Water enlarges, Dundee slips by an age
Into its land before the lights come on.
Pale, mystic lamps lean on the river-road
Bleaching the city's lunar after-image,
And there's the moon, and there's the setting sun.

The rail bridge melts in a dramatic haze.
Slow visibility – a long train floats
Through a stopped shower's narrow waterways
Above rose-coloured river, dappled motes
In the eye and the narrow piers half-real
Until a cloud somewhere far in the west
Mixes its inks and draws iron and stone
In epic outlines, black and literal,
Now it is simple, weathered, plain, immodest
In waterlight and late hill-hidden sun.

High water adds freshwater-filtered salt
To the aquatic mirrors, a thin spice
That sharpens light on Middle Bank, a lilt
In the reflected moon's analysis.
Mud's sieved and drained from pewter into gold.
Conjectural infinity's outdone
By engineering, light and hydrous fact,
A waterfront that rises fold by fold
Into the stars beyond the last of stone,
A city's elements, local, exact.

THE TAY BRIDGE

L. A. Lefevre

On through the storm! The rushing, swaying
    train
Chased by the demon winds and mad with fear,
Up to the cold, white moon that will not hear
Sends shrieks for pity as it flies in pain.
On through the night! The iron sinews strain
Freighted with human lives, the Firth is near,
And in the tempest surging wild and drear
The wind-swept waters warning shout in vain.
On to the Bridge! The giant girders groan,
They tremble, fall! then under the wide sky
No trace of aught but ruin, and the moan
Of waves that roll o'er death and agony.
Bright hopes! Fair dreams! Was it for this alone
Ye blossomed in the hearts that silent lie?

THE CARSE
Lewis Spence

It is a thousand sunsets since I lay
In many-birded Gowrie, and did know
Its shadow for my soul, that passionate Tay
Out of my heart did flow.

The immortal hour the hate of time defies.
Men of my loins a million years away
And in their blood the Tay.

THE TAY MOSES
Kathleen Jamie

What can I fashion
for you but a woven
creel of river –
rashes, a golden
oriole's nest, my gift
wrought from the Firth –

and choose my tide: either
the flow, when, watertight
you'll drift to the uplands –
my favourite hills; held safe
in eddies, where salmon, wisdom
and guts withered in spawn,
rest between moves – that
slither of body as you were born –

or the ebb, when the water
will birl you to snag
on reeds, the river-
pilot leaning over the side:
'*Name o God!*' and you'll change hands:
tractor-man, grieve, farm-wife
who takes you into her
competent arms

even as I drive, slamming
the car's gears,
spitting gravel on tracks
down between berry-fields,
engine still racing, the door wide
as I run toward her, crying
LEAVE HIM! Please,
it's okay, he's mine.

THE LIGHTHOUSE

Anne Stevenson

Though I did not intend
on my journey that it should end
at this lighthouse and town
surrounded by tidewater's flat brown
halo of muddy sand
opening and closing like a hand,
clearly, on looking back, I see
the road led here inevitably.

With its litter of feathers and shells, it bends
on further, blends
with blue water further than I can see.
And is what will be.
The bay – so beautiful.
I – only its animal.
And the lighthouse, ever unsatisfied,
Glutted in the tide.

THE TAY (EXTRACT)
David Millar

Dundee, thy din is silent here. The clang
Of ponderous hammers, and the ceaseless sound
Of mighty engines, on whose heavings hang
The weal of multitudes—the stunning round
Of myriad spindles, shaking the firm ground—
Trade's restless tramp—the sailors' loud 'Ye-ho!'
Are voiceless all, as hushed in sleep profound:
Nought tells of noisy bustle but its show—
Sails, smoking chimneys round, and hurryings to and fro!
'Tis a strange motley sight, but grand withal—
Ten thousand crowded homes, so pent and piled
Incongruous, jarring roofs, and chimneys tall—
Red, blue, and grey—and all so grimly soiled.
Towers, churches, steeples, pressed upon and coiled
By winding labyrinths of huddled walls
And glistening windows, where the eye is foiled
To trace out order; for where'er it falls
Are houses, houses still—spires, chimney-stalks, and halls.
Beyond is simple beauty steeped in light,
The golden light of summer's brilliant sky.

A VIEW OF THE TAY

Lorraine McCann

A line, edgy and flexible,
    corrupted by wooden legs,
    and stung by pin-pricks of dull orange
    that bleed downwards and fade,
to black.

The river smells chill, sounds wet.
This is where we dumped the body.
This is where it came back.

Putting your hand in this is like being alive
    it's a nothingness so cold that it burns.
Drowning is beautiful – she didn't drown.
But those tangy pools of mirrored neon
    are her eyes.

MIST
Gordon Meade

for Stewart Syme

A forest of pine trees felled
by mist, uprooted by vapour, and rendered
invisible by particles of water,

suspended in air. Cattle isolated,
removed from their herds in pockets of fog.
Ewes losing their lambs. Loosed

from their mothers' moorings,
wrapped in damp blankets, their shallow
bleats carry like foghorns through

the fading light. Beneath the city's
twin bridges, a river of seals flows slowly
onwards, water confined by banks.

As it reaches the estuary, moved
by the moon, it relinquishes the illusive land,
for the salt-water clarity of sea.

CROSSING THE TAY BRIDGE
Lydia Robb

A vast blue wash
from bridge to sky

and a solitary boat tugs
a glitter of fishscales,

the estuary, a map
with no boundaries.

Tayport whitens its bones
In a sea of haar.

Rust-red stalactites weld
themselves into a hard-edged echo.

BROUGHTY FERRY
William Montgomerie

The lamps across the river
are lilies of light
rooted with fire

The evening star
is a windflower of light

The crescent moon
holds the apple of darkness
in a glass

Three fishermen
are talking by the drawn-up boats

They know the dark river
and the sea beyond

DAWN
Brenda Shaw

I wake and hear the wet grey wind
blowing
blowing
along the Tay
the wild grey Tay
along the Green
and past my gate
It never stops, will never stop
forever more
forever more
They'll bury me
with the cold grey wind
blowing,
blowing.

TAY 5
Harvey Holton

Empy the wheat shovel the haunles grown cauld
winter the wheel will deny the wudden blade
the coorse yird tae dig, the city tae beild.
Derk noo the factory oan the watters edge
empy the docks noo whaur the shovel swung.
Blinter the licht whaur the deid ship sailed
nae grain noo lies warm in the hold.
Navigation, triangulation wiz wance said
frae Deid Mans Bank tae be the shield,
the shape that held the watters pledge:
Spring tides in spokes o fire are hung.
Again the thistle tae the waa is nailed.

TAY 6
Harvey Holton

Fire formit the shape whaur nets dry.
The guid fire biggit in places as hames
whaur nae kirk wundie keeks oan skin coverins
caulkit an clinker biggit in their ain worship.
Strecht the pines, Lodge Pole or Larch, try
fur the lift tae reach. The sternies kaimes
the wuiddin dwam, the man makit nummerins
that mind the path, the richt tune tae trip.
Hard oan the watter the solid laund slides

THE TAY BRIDGE
George Colburn

I stood upon the Scottish 'Bridge of Sighs' —
That wondrous product of a great man's dream;
I saw its piers and stately girders rise
In airy grandeur from the mighty stream
That pour its dark and murky waves between
Banks famous in the warlike days of yore,
Where now the towers of trade and learning gleam;
And o'er the broad expanse this bridge did soar,
Like some gigantic chain, linking shore to shore.

How slowly, yet how gracefully it sprang
From out the bosom of the flowing deep,
So slow that but for sounding hammers' clang,
Men might have thought that, in their hours of sleep,
Those tiny workers of the mighty deep,
That raise the island from the ocean cave,
Had laid its base where unknown monsters creep,
And proudly piled its head above the wave —
The waters and the winds alike to brave.

And on this giant bridge men came to gaze,
With something mixed of pleasure and of awe;
And though they spoke their wonder and their praise,
They scarce could grasp the mighty work they saw —
It seemed that nature's self and nature's law
Alike were subject to man's grasping power,
Whose bonds, alas! were weak as common straw;
For shivered in one dread, disastrous hour
Were all his subtle skill and giant power.

I see the fatal gap, the shattered form,
And that dark stream, whose cold and sullen wave
Received the victims of that deadly storm;
Around each broken pier its waters lave,
Deep, dark, and hungry as the yawning grave —
Low, deeply murmuring the forget-me-not

Of those who died without one arm to save.
An air of sadness still pervades this spot,
Which time may chasten though it quenches not.

TAYSIDE VILLANELLE

Forbes Browne

Waves roar and surge then slither on the sand,
Blown wrack and branches mingle in the spray,
The tide repeats its inroads on the land.

Leaves, litter, feathers fly at every hand,
Wind rises with the dying of the day;
Waves roar and surge then slither on the sand.

The wind sends whirlpools spinning from the strand,
Blackheaded gulls take shelter where they may,
The tide repeats its inroads on the land.

Across the estuary night clouds band
Together, make the dimming of the day;
Waves roar and surge then slither on the sand.

Upon the dunes the marram sways but stands
As wind builds up and sweeps across the bay;
The tide repeats its inroads on the land.

In darkening sky geese write an unknown hand,
The wind helps speed the skeins along their way.
Waves roar and surge then slither on the sand;
The tide repeats its inroads on the land.

GREAT TAY OF THE WAVES

Lewis Spence

O that yon river micht nae mair
    Rin through the channels o' my sleep;
My bluid has felt its tides owre sair,
    Its waves hae drooned my dreams owre deep.

O why should Tay be a' my day
    And Buddon links be a' my nicht,
The warld o' a' my walks be gray
    Wi' yon far sands' unwarldly licht?

As haars the windless waters find
    The unguarded instant falls a prey
To sakeless shadows o' the mind,
    And a' my life runs back to Tay.

Deep in the saul the early scene –
    Ah, let him play wi' suns wha can,
The cradle's pented on the een,
    The native airt resolves the man!

A DAY AT THE SEASIDE

John Glenday

We're out in my father's boat and he's fishing.
He's fishing until the daylight goes.
It's the end of the season and I'm in the stern
to watch for the ebb that would pull us

out past the Buddon Light and the mouth of the river.
But I'm not watching the tide,
I'm watching him as he fishes, because I've never
seen him so focussed before – so engaged.

It's as if the fish had hooked him. Then just
as he makes his final cast, an oyster catcher calls
far out across the water. Far out across
the water an oyster catcher calls

just once, and then just once again, and then its silence calls.
The hurt lies not in the cross, but in the nails.

ODE TO THE NEW OLD TAY BRIDGE
W.N. Herbert

The Storm Fiend did loudly bray,
Because ninety lives had been taken away,
On the last Sabbath day of 1879,
Which will be remember'd for a very long time.
(William MacGonagall)

Twas in the clammy autumn of 2003
I was commissioned by some madmen at the BBC
to write aboot you, rickety auld Tay railbridge
(a prospect as cheery as inhabiting a fridge),
and a turbid revelation wiz granted unto me –
disturbin fur a Scotsman afore he's hud his tea –
that William McGonagall, wha wrote aboot you furst,
wiz no a woeful poet but a thingummy far worse:
a juggernaut of doggerel, the laureate from Hell,
an icon of his era like tae Issie K. Brunel.

While Isambard build iron boats the same size as the ocean
McGonagall wrote rusty verse of abyssal proportion
devoted to catastrophe domestic or abroad –
nae massacre or forest fire this man wad not applaud.
The fact that he wiz abstinent made me begin tae think
total calamity his substitute fur drink;
the fact that he wiz obstinant, tho brainless as a midge,
made me think aboot this Storm Fiend that he sez attacked
     the bridge,
for this wiz his disaster, his wee Pompeii-on-Tay:
the bridge fell doon, a haill train drooned, all on a Hogmanay...

When one surveys yir predecessor, built by Thomas Bouch,
there's an inclination to adopt a tight defensive crouch,
but it disnae tak a Storm Fiend tae plant some gelignite
like it disnae tak a genius tae pen a load o shite.
McGonagall wiz guilty, and God wiz fair but hard:
he possessed yir every atom wi the spirit of wir bard.
Each girder is a rib, and every rail a tooth,

every bolt's an eyeball, and yir redbrick piles...'Forsooth!'
we'll hear you cry as we rattle intae toon,
'Why must they cross the River Tay while I have my
    troosers doon?'

NOTE: The first Tay Bridge, as McGonagall tells us, fell in 1879.
Its successor was built in 1887, and is still (touch wood) in service.

THE ESTUARY
Gordon Meade

The silvery Tay is lead today, or a sheet
of ice in the process of melting. It is not moving.
There is no hint of it flowing, as it should,

towards the sea. It is a bit like all of us,
stuck in our different ways of mourning. As ever,
I take the easy way out and pick up a pen;

what doesn't get formed into a poem, at least
will have seen the light of day before being binned.
Others keep their feelings hidden. When the sun-

light hits the surface of the water, suddenly
all the clichés come true and it does turn to silver.
On another day, gallons of the stuff will make

their way rapidly to the mouth. Maybe some
day we, also, will be able to share the grief that,
for the moment, both unites us and destroys.

THE MUDTOWER
(TAYPORT, FIFE, 1 JANUARY, 1975)
Anne Stevenson

And again, without snow, a new year.
As for hundreds of years, thousands of years, the air
returns the child-blue rage of the river.
Six swans rise aloud from the estuary,
ferrying tremendous souls to the pond by the playground.
They're coming for me! No, I'm part of the scenery.
They fly low, taking no interest in migratory ladies.

The stone town stumbles down hill to untidy mudflats –
high square houses shivering in windows, the street of shops,
the church and clocktower, school, the four worn pubs
artfully spaced between dry rows of cottages.
Then council flats, fire station, rusty gasometer,
timber-yard baying its clean smell of pinewood;
grass, swings, mud…the wilted estuary.

You could say that the winter's asleep in the harbour's arm.
Two sloops with their heads on their backs
       are sleeping there peacefully.
Far out in the tide's slum, in the arm of the sand-spit,
the mudtower wades in the giving and taking water.
Its uses, if it ever had uses, have been abandoned.
The low door's a mouth. Slit eyes stab the pinnacle.
Its lovethrust is up from the mud it seems to be made of.
Surely it's alive and hibernating, Pictish or animal.
The seabirds can hear it breathing in its skin or shrine.
How those lighthouses, airing their bones on the coast,
hate the mudtower. They hold their bright messages aloft
like saints bearing scriptures.

As the water withdraws, the mudtower steps out on the land.
Watch the fierce, driven, hot-looking
scuttlings of the redshanks, the beaks of the oystercatchers.
Struggle and panic. Struggle and panic.
Mud's rituals resume. The priest-gulls flap to the kill.

Now high flocks of sandpipers, wings made of sunlight,
flicker as snow flickers, blown from those inland hills.

2
THE TOWN

TAODUNUM

Arthur Johnston

(TRANSLATED FROM THE LATIN BY ROBERT CRAWFORD)

Veteran admiral of the windy Tay,
Commanding a great Firth whose shores stretch out
To where invading Vikings left their bones,
The marble palaces of Genoa,
The pyramids of Memphis, count for nothing
Compared to you. You trump all Gargara
For sheer abundance, and for seamanship
Out-sail Liburnia, Cnidus, even Venice.
Your boys are braver than the lads of Sparta.
Your councillors out-argue even Rome's.
Only the ignorant pretend your name
Derives prosaically from Dun Tay;
Your true root's far more nimbly classical;
Dundee, Dei Donum, God's Gift.

00:00: LAW TUNNEL

(Leased to the Scottish Mushroom Company
after its closure in 1927)
Don Paterson

(i)

In the airy lull
between the wars
they cut the rails
and closed the doors

on the stalled freight:
crate on crate
of blood and earth –
the shallow berth

of the innocents,
their long room
stale and tense
with the same dream

(ii)

Strewn among
the ragged queue –
the snoring king
and his retinue,

Fenrir, Pol Pot,
Captain Oates
and the leprechauns –
are the teeth, the bones

and begging-cup
of the drunken piper.
The rats boiled up
below the sleepers

(iii)

The crippled boy
of Hamelin
pounds away
at the locked mountain

waist-deep in thorn
and all forlorn,
he tries to force
the buried doors

I will go to my mother
and sing of my shame
I will grow up to father
the race of the lame

BLACKNESS ROAD

Kate Armstrong

This uphill street's a chimney for the town
A colour-chart of what was made and done.

For centuries the reek of the age of coal
coated the foundry, tenements, two schools and a mill,

painted the city black, the rabbit-brown
sandstone faces black as basalt until one by one

they were knocked down, unwanted, set on fire;
the homes remain. Year upon year

the giants fell. Still there are tiny shops
nesting below the dwellings. A bus creeps

coughing up, does its best, drops off its few.
Great gaps in the buildings now

let light wash in like the stirring sea
into Fingal's Cave. Stone breathes. The windows shine back blue.

SELF-PORTRAIT IN THE DARK

(WITH CIGARETTE)

Colette Bryce

To sleep, perchance
to dream? No chance:
it's 4 a.m. and I'm wakeful
as an animal,
caught between your presence and the lack.
This is the realm insomniac.
On the window seat, I light a cigarette
from a slim flame and monitor the street –
a stilled film, bathed in amber,
softened now in the wake of a downpour.

Beyond the daffodils
on Magdalen Green, there's one slow vehicle
pushing its beam along the Riverside Drive,
a sign of life;
and two months on
from 'moving on'
your car, that you haven't yet picked up,
waits, spattered in raindrops like bubble wrap.
Here, I could easily go off
on a riff

on how cars, like pets, look a little like their owners
but I won't 'go there',
as they say in America,
given it's a clapped-out Nissan Micra…
And you don't need to know that
I've been driving it illegally at night
in the lamp-lit silence of this city
– you'd only worry –
or, worse, that Morrissey
is jammed in the tape deck now and for eternity;

no. It's fine, all gleaming hubcaps,
seats like an upright, silhouetted couple;
from the dashboard, the wink
of that small red light I think
is an in-built security system.
In a poem
it could represent a heartbeat or a pulse.
Or loneliness: its vigilance.
Or simply the lighthouse-regular spark
of someone, somewhere, smoking in the dark.

BROCHTY FERRY: A SONG OF SUBURBIA
Joseph Lee

'Come unto these yellow sands.' – Ariel's Song in the Tempest.

Whan City Merchants, cool an' cute,
Hae fortunes made frae jam or jute,
They flee, to 'scape the smeek an' soot
    Awa to Brochty Ferry.

To 'scape the smeek an' but the tax,
(Our laws are shure a trifle lax).
They tak' the honey, leave the wax
    These Nabobs o' the Ferry.

An' thus we see braw villas stand
Wi' whigmaleeries on ilk hand,
As raised by some enchanter's wand
    Round bonnie Brochty Ferry.

The Castle – oor ain stout Gibraltar,
Lat's see the foe wad dare assault her !
I'se warrant ye we'd mak' them swalter
    Wi' gun fire frae the Ferry.

An' gin the Frenchman try to land,
There's mines be hodden i' the sand,
Will send them clean to – Styx's strand
    Blawn straight frae Brochty Ferry.

Why gang to Spas to sip the water,
To mak' yer bodies lean or fatter,
Or add a cubit to yer stat're ?
    Just ye try Brochty Ferry.

Into the surf the bathers swarm,
The day is fair – the w-at-er's – w-w-a-rm ;
Sips o' saut Tay will work sma' harm,
    When bathing at the Ferry.

Ye Lunnon fouks, wi' muckle pride,
Doon Rotten Raw are wont to glide,
Did'st ever hae a donkey-ride
    On sands o' Brochty Ferry ?

Just pey, an' mount an' ride awa',
Skelp him behind – tug at his jaw ;
If he gae nae back'ard ye may craw
    Fu' crouse at Brochty Ferry.

Behold yon younglings, void o' care,
O' saft white sand build castles fair,
(Tho' but an equal fate to share
Wi' mine, that builded i' the air)
    Natheless, let us be merrie !

An' mony an auld salt, frank an' free,
After lang tossin' on the sea,
Finds haven, whare he fain wad be,
    Doon by at Brochty Ferry.

Sunbrunt, an' mar'd wi' seam an' scar,
Sign o' strange journeyings afar –
Peace to them whan they cross the bar
    At last frae Brochty Ferry.

DUNDEE
John Burnside

The streets are waiting for a snow
that never falls:
too close to the water,
too muffled in the afterwarmth of jute,
the houses on Roseangle
opt for miraculous frosts
and the feeling of space that comes
in the gleam of day
when you step outside for the milk
or the morning post
and it seems as if a closeness in the mind
had opened and flowered:
the corners sudden and tender, the light immense,
the one who stands here proven after all.

DENS ROAD MARKET
A. D. Foote

That morning I arrived too early:
Half of the stalls were shrouded in sackcloth
And a handful
Of children, darting about and laughing,
Were the only other visitors.
At a counter
I ordered tea in a polystyrene cup
The milk-jug was empty
'Help yourself to the Coffee-mate!'
(I thought I was being addressed as 'mate')
And sat down to see what
Would happen.
A yard or two away was a wire compound
Full of books in a various stages of decay.
Then I noticed a mousy little
Woman going among them
'No, I'm not the proprietress
But come in and look if you want…'
I looked – a Hebrew textbook
Heavily annotated in crude ball-point:
No priceless jewels, whether of prose or verse,
No passport to the thousand palaces…
The little woman had disappeared:
No one was looking, and no one cared.
The children burst out laughing
At a Peke in a green collar.
I went out through the fire exit.
In the street, making one hell of a din,
A road-breaking machine went trundling by.

2ND DOLDRUM (ELEPHANTS' GRAVEYARD)

W. N. Herbert

Whaur ur yi Dundee? Whaur's yir Golem buriit?
Whaur doon yir pendies lurks it?
Broon brick, eldscoorit, timedustchoakit,
blin windies – whaur's MaGonnagal's hert?
Creh o seagulls echoes thru closies' lugs:
nithin but'iz hertsherds, shatterit, deidtrootdreh,
nithin but vishuns o lehburers deean.

Eh kent yi i thi street; Peddie Street
whaur boarn an raisd in tenements
ma sowelclert sheppit; Eh spoattit yi
certin a wheelbarra ower cobblies
(ower tarmaccadum and undir um's thi cobblestanes,
deid buriit jaabanes o yir weans' hopes),
Eh saw yi in grey overalls, een deid an blank,
heid bulletgrey an taursmearit, durt
clung til yir een,
and indivisibul fae yir past,
oot o thi fremms o photygraphs
waulkin weldit tae wheelbarra,
haunds soldert tae toil, an nae rest.

Ghaist o thi Thurties, Dundee whan thi Daith cam doon,
grey cinders descendin, meldit wi claiths an dreams,
Dundee whan Amerika fell,
Dundee whan thi Depreshun cam owerseas
an bidit, an restit in oor faithirs' braces –
oor flatbunnits! oor bandylegs! oor rickets!
Waulkin uppa street, a deid, a ghostie,
a passedby, a damnit, a wurkir –
ghaist restless and nivir kennin green.

A DREAM-VISIT TO A
HAUNT OF MY BOYHOOD
Robert Leighton

Between Dundee and Invergowrie kirk,
   There is a lonely spot owergrown wi' brier,
Some scranky twigs of ash, and some o' birk,
   Whar maistly aye the sun is shinin' clear.

And, scatter'd round, gray rocks, like ruins, lie –
   They ha'e a grandeur in their very gloom;
Lang wither'd grass shoots upwards, rank and high,
   Through bristly whins that aften are in bloom.

Ah, 'tis a bonnie spot! I aft gaed there,
   When Sabbath stillness hung ower all aroun',
And no a voice disturb'd the hallow'd air,
   Except the birdie warblin' ower its tune.

There, leanin' on a rock, the hail half day,
   I eagerly a list'ning ear wad keep,
To hear the hollow gurglin' o' the Tay,
   As 'tween the rocks at intervals she'd creep.

Last nicht I wander'd to that lonely scene;
   Though 'twas the dead o' nicht, the sky was clear;
But nicht grew day-the orb o' day did sheene –
   And never did a day mair bricht appear!

There was the rock-I almost ca'd it mine,
   Because it was the rock I used to choose –
And there I sat me doon for auld-lang-syne,
   A while upon the by-gane days to muse.

A' things around me here reflections bring:
   Here lie the big gray stanes, owergrown wi' fog:
There lies the wither'd ash-puir broken thing –
   The very tree whareon I used to shog!

And there's the *figured* stane – dim to the sicht –
  I thocht a relic o' some ither days,
And pu'd, and pu'd, and pu'd wi' a' my micht,
  And did, at last, succeed that stane to raise.

Beneath, the sod was damp – white roots o' grass –
  Wirms in their holes were drawing in their tails –
Across and slantways glary streaks did pass,
  That lookit like the slimy marks o' snails.

There, stane, just as I left you still ye stand;
  And there's the mark o' whar ye lay before:
Maybe some grannie, dead, could gi'en, aff hand,
  Lang screeds 'bout you o' legendary lore.

But what's the meanin' o' sae mony birds?
  There ne'er was half sae mony on thir braes!
And hark! I think I hear some whisperin' wirds: –
  'Come let us bear him up,' a blackie says.

This was the biggest blackie e'er I saw:
  Had his neb but been black, as it was red,
I'd taen him for some muckle hoodie-craw, –
  He'd funds o' mither-wit in yon big head!

Then did he gi'e his neck a gracefu' bend,
  And, haupin', came in-ower, no ony shy: –
'I'll shortly tell,' says he, 'what we intend;
  Auld friend, we're gaun to lift ye to the sky!

'There will ye get a cloud whereon to rest –
  There will ye get a lyre whereon to play –
There, on your head, ye'll get a flowery crest,
  And float about the air the lee-lang day.

'And should ye wish to get into the mune,
  Or ony ither orb, a while to bide;
Sune as the wish comes in your head, as sune
  Towards the place desired ye'll saftly glide.

'And dinna think, because ye canna see,
   That in the clouds nae earthly beauties are;
There, plenty of our kind, woods, burnies be –
   Than earthly beauties they are bonnier far!

'If ye to wander through the woods incline –
   If rocky dingles should be your desire –
There's mony a place whereat the twa combine,
   And send a thousand echoes to the lyre!'

Thus spak' the blackie, and he ended here;
   Then maikently and gracefully turn'd round,
And noddit to the whins and to the brier,
   And then I heard a chirpin' kind o' sound.

Of ilka singin' bird in Scotia's land,
   Around about the blackie cam' a pair;
And ilka pair between them had a wand,
   Whereon they bore me lichtly through the air.

But how we landed at our journey's end
   Is what I winna tak' in hand to say;
For here a darkness round us did extend,
   And nicht was nicht, and was nae langer day!

NEW HOMES
Margaret Gillies Brown

These crumbling northern nesting-barns must go
Where swallows have for centuries been drawn
From tigered veldt and Drakensbergs they know
On flights paths gened from generations gone
To where the blackthorn whitens into flower
And grass is April-green with sun and shower.

I've watched these scythe-birds from firecrest dawn
Gathering mud from every rainy pool,
Wheel about the marsh, above the lawn,
Dive below lintels into sudden cool;
There on the crossbeam rafters come to rest,
Under curving pantiles build a nest.

These old red roofs are now beyond repair,
These walls of stone in every shape and shade
Must meet their fate, (the JCB's loud blare)
That once with skill, the caring craftsman made;
Yet modern days and modern ways must be,
New things grow, although it saddens me.

But see – across the fields, the phoenix rise
From rubble on our nearest neighbour's place
Silver-white it leans against the skies,
Down-winged and high it has an airy grace;
Here tall-cabbed tractors are now housed at night
And swallows build fresh nests at greater height.

For nothing lives if it becomes time-trapped
And everything must die that won't adapt.

MARY SHELLEY ON
BROUGHTY FERRY BEACH
Robert Crawford

One small boat tugs the enormous corpse inshore
Towards waiting locals. A lad opens up its mouth
And wades inside, clutching a flensing tool
For blubber. Piece by hacked-off piece

Men deconstruct the outcast zeppelin body,
Carting lumps back to beachfront cottages –
Sturdy food and good oil for the winter.
Harpoons glint in the candlelight.

Safe home, the men of Broughty Ferry take
Their sweet uncorseted wifes to bed, or croon
Shanties to bairns beside toys made of teeth.
The Tay flows quiet. Dundee's lights wink their yellow.

A sad girl walks from the beach, carefully picking
Her steps as she sneaks past a leftover eye
Flung on the sand, and other small last bits
Of monster littering the promenade.

MONIFIETH BEACH

Valerie Cuming

Grey early-morning mist
Gives way to an orange sun
Like a beach ball
Lying on the sand.

The tide is far out.
When we go for a walk
There will be few people
Along the empty bay,
Now bereft of dunes and
Marram grass.
The spring tide has done its
Work with chisel-like precision
Cutting the dunes,
Exposing the rubble core.

Once, not long ago,
Profuse vegetation
Gave pleasure to the eye;
Greater periwinkle and Russian vine,
Meadowsweet, redcurrant and the dog rose
All grew in the shelter of the dunes,
And delirious children
Roly-poly'd down the bank.

Now barriers and warning notices are seen:
This way is closed.
Pass only at your risk …
The other path leads to red
Flags and mortar shells.

Walk at your peril, except
At Christmas and New Year.
No guns over the holidays.
The sea, however,
Knows no rules.

MAGDALEN GREEN
Donald Campbell

Dounby the Magdalen Green
I think I hear ye singing
on the dark side of my dreams
as the winter nicht descends.
Your voice is warm and gentle
in a world that's cauld and mean
and the darkness haps me tichtly
dounby the Magdalen Green.

Dounby the Magdalen Green
I feel that ye're aye near me
though there's nathing to be seen
on the road I walk my lane.
Oh, the wind is roaring rarely
and the nicht is snell and keen
but the paths are unco slippery
dounby the Magdalen Green.

Oh, here I am a stranger
new landed frae the sea
and my ship she lies at anchor
in the harbour of Dundee
and I'm ettling sair to tell ye
what I've done and where I've been
though I ken I canna find ye here
dounby the Magdalen Green.

Dounby the Magdalen Green
as I rise up in the morning
the sunlicht's brichtest scene
winna bring ye back again.
Though the river's running sweetly
and the air is clear and clean,
your spirit canna reach me nou
dounby the Magdalen Green.

GOING HOME
Val Warner

Soon, winter will black out all afternoon.
Even at 3 o'clock, on sky's spring tide,
the day's a sick rose, flushed and dying fast;
heaven's a blush rose, reddened past belief.
Last of the gaudy summer daze…may still
transcend some of November's golden days,
early on in the month's dying fall, still

I shan't get home before the light has gone.
Over the Tay, clouds are lit up, wine-dark

over the hills, over the water. Still

welling nostalgia for the daylight drowns
all that worry. It's going as I look.
How long will our seasons' cycle last? Four

or five…miles on after the dark wood where
the bus turns – in the middle of nowhere
called Hazelton Crossroads – slyly my stride
starts to shrink, going home. My room's that far

horizon? Now light runs out on me, but
half-way there. Wellingtons slur on leafmould,
fudging the gun-shot rending through beech masts.
I fear it will be night before I'm there.

DUNDEE SONNET 6
George T. Watt

Dreich, an ower uised word fur Scottish weither,
grey lift hingin ower the toun like a sair heid,
syver lids wheeched oot on the Lochee road,
whummled tenements, dreips drappin frae the rhone
tell o the wild blatter fit tore throu the toun.

Frae ae turn on the brae ae lang luik aistward shows,
grey sea an bleck cloud knit thegither bi dairk threids
taiglin the daylicht ahint its hodden waive,
thare's nae birdsang this shell shocked simmers morn,
nae gowden trumpets fur this apocalyptic dawn.

Nae drouth abune the causy tae raise this disjaskit dey
nae wun abune the pairk tae flutter amang the trees,
but ae buddleia buss tummlin pollen in the air,
gaed licht tae sudden thochts, like butterflees.

BROUGHTY FERRY
Douglas Dunn

Under the eaves, Elysian icicles
Taper towards stilled drips. In my garden
A naked birch looks lacquered by a hand
Expert in Christmas things or fairyland
Translations. Clever frost has hardened lace
On spiderwebs and shrubs. It has blinded glass
All over the planthouse, and spelled a rose
Into a shuttered bud.

On Broughty Ferry's mansioned slopes, houses
Address the sun I set my eye by, stepping
Through wintry trees, and there's an hour to go
Before the roselight comes to fill the sky.
Yesterday's money celebrates its stone
With watery, cold, imperial
Throwbacks to somewhere else, a hesitant
Refrigerated Orient.

I came home through the Country Bus Station
Eager for half-past-one and views from Fife.
A winey down-and-out, his poly bag
No bundle for a shouldered stick, outstared
Distaste and sentiment, a holly sprig
Defiant in his cap of weathered tweed.
A well-dressed mother with her hand-held son
Resented being there and looked away.

A simpleton went through a dance routine
Shuffling on the cold tiles of the alcove,
Pulling the faces of a mind content
With suffering's low comedy.
A one-legged pigeon hopped between the queues
With messages from Orphic pauperdom.
Cherubic sparrows huddled in their rags.
Policewoman struggled with a runaway.

Inspectors helped a blind man on a bus,
Then when their backs were turned, got off again,
Chasing white probes with thirst or memory.
Young men and women swaggered on the platform,
Loitering, discontent and ghetto-blasting.
Old women, frightened by the depot's
Aroma'd roar, fingered their counted change
Or checked their travel passes, passports home.

My comfortable, mind-aggrandized visions
Melt in the light and then my eyes play tricks
Or beauty tricks my eyes into conceit:
I won't disfigure loveliness I see
With an avoidance of its politics.
Although the silvered rust of docken seed
Shows it has none, nor whitened, brittle grass,
That isn't true of Broughty Ferry's stone,

Improved by roselight's neutral flawlessness,
Dismissing what I think of what I see
Into a stunned perfection, remote,
Depopulated and complacent.
I think of incomes and prosperity.
It comes to Wednesday's rhymed phrase
Holding together versions of events,
Significance that beauty can't erase.

A DUNDEE PASTORAL

William J. Rae

Are Phyllis and Corydon still to be seen
A-tending their flocks on Magdalen Green,
While up Shepherd's Loan, on his oaten flute,
Does Thyrsis compete with the clack of the jute?

In Peep o' Day Lane when cocks start to crow,
Does that prompt the cattle in Cowgate to low?
Do Lilybank milkmaids, with footfall soft,
Pick flowers on the way to their work in Blackscroft?

Are there mussels to tempt the hungry peasant
Who travels Isles Lane to scale Mount Pleasant?
Or should he go off to Strawberrybank,
The place to enjoy a picnicking prank?

Is this the season to cast away pride
And all go a-maying in Meadowside,
Or else to relinquish the cares of trade,
Sporting with Amaryllis in Blackshade?

NIGHT WIND, DUNDEE

Anne Stevenson

At sundown, a seaforce that gulls rode or fell through.
The small snow is surf. Eddies of strong air
Swarm up old tenements. Listen! My window's late
Rat-tat-tat guns back at who and whose enemy
Milked the sky's agates, polished its ebony.
Warm rooms are lit up in bare blocks of concrete.
Someone's ripped cobwebs from a great vault's rafters,
Revealing a moonface, a starfield,
Barbarian Orion crucified in God's heaven.

SOOTH ROAD
David Phillips

Yaseti ken a lassie crehed Mary —
Sarah-Ann-Jane in Tipperary;
Playin' tig in the Boag in wir baries;
That's whut Eh liked aboot Sooth Road.

She hud six sisters, brithers three;
Father poached rabbits fir the femily;
Mither felt nae need fur Vitamin E,
That's whut she liked aboot Sooth Road.

We sellt jeely-jars t'git t'the show;
Coppers got wiz inti Joe's Casino;
Mair fun in the front than in the back row!
An' that's whut we liked aboot Sooth Road.

Setturday nicht's intertainmint wuz free;
We'd stand ootside the hostelries;
The drunks come fleein' oot backarties,
An' that's whut we liked aboot Sooth Road.

Her father wuz a real hard cha',
It took three polis tae drag him awa'
Whin he'd hud an extry joog ur twa;
Hardest man in the Sooth Road.

Well, Mary-etc., an' me grous big;
She wuz teachin' me the Irish Jig —
Till Dad learned Eh wuz boarn *ootside* the Brig;
A tearful ta-ta in Sooth Road!

Now, Tipperary's went a' swank,
Fuhll o' fowk wi money in the bank
An' a car ut the door wi' petrol in the tank;
Whut's happened tae Sooth Road?

Worse, in pubs the strehdent tones
O' groups blare inti mecrephones …
Ach, but they still keep a coarner fur 'the bones'
An' that's whut Eh like aboot Sooth Road!

THE CAPTAIN'S HOUSE
(1 WEST SOMERVILLE PLACE, DUNDEE)
David Dick

Five minutes to Dundee, and three to Hilltown shops,
And half-way up a steeply southward-facing hill,
An advantageous situation for a house
The Captain must have thought, recently retired from sea.
And past the gate, a great convenience for its time,
There ran a railway track, with carriages drawn up
By rope and stationary engine on the hill,
An early British railway, just the very thing
After a tiring day in town. Also this track
Divided off from Dudhope Castle lands, a plot
Suitably sized for a building, and with extensive view
Far over the river to St. Andrews' huddled spires,
Easily seen on clear days after rain. And so
In 1834 the Captain made his plans
To build a handsome house in classic style, although
Already passé in the South, just lately seized
With Gothic grandiose romance, turrets and towers.
But here the Captain wanted mainly practical
Douce domesticity, with elegance enough
To show a man of modest taste and common sense.

The house is square; the front door central with a hint
Of fluted columns either side. Above the door
French windows lead onto a balcony from which
The Captain scanned the garden foredeck just as if
At sea. To right and left on ground and upper floors
Windows of rooms, unornamented and alike,
Yet not a symmetry exact; the left hand rooms
Have each bow windows giving extra light and view,
Attractive feature of the house. And at the top
Accommodation for a small domestic staff,
In attic rooms with dormer windows in the roof.

The Captain lived here thirty years and saw
The railway closed, with a diversion round the hill,
And hospital extensions built across the track.
He watched the town sprout smoky stacks of factories,
Converting oil and jute to coarse convenient sacks,
Which then exported back to India and Bengal
Made comfortable profits for a very few
And filth for many more. Over a hundred years
The blinded house peered just above the fog, itself
Almost unsmirched. But now the stacks no longer smoke;
Thanks to enlightened legislation and control,
The Captain's house today enjoys its ancient view
Across the newly smokeless city and the Tay.

SOUTH UNION STREET BY NIGHT

Norval Scrimgeour

When ghosts of twilight throng the street,
　　And softly tolls the steeple bell;
When every pipe is passing sweet,
　　And every fusee casts a spell;
When 'mid the shadows of the night
Cigar and cigarette burn bright.

I hold it sacred to the hour,
　　A place where visions come and go;
Where I can see the heavy tower
　　Darken against the fading glow.
A subtle something steals like rain,
And then I see the Strand again.

Now here, now there the cab lights dart,
　　Shrill voices echo in the gloom;
And now through curtains still apart
　　I see some homely firelit room.
But yet familiar sounds and sights
Have vanished in the Lyceum lights.

HAIKU FOR THE LAW

David Fyans

I LAY DOWN TO DREAM IN THE SHADOW OF THE HILL AND THE HILL DREAMS BACK

WARP

Val Warner

Meaningless to ask what a city's like…
even the town of the three Js – jute, jam
and journalism – although lost for words. Hell –
I've lost her spiel's thread '…the West End,
where they built their piles, after making them…
betraying their hands to the mills' treadmills.
Jam tomorrow? Pie in Tay sky, that frames

a Latin quarter now. The warm north May…
students in sweeping dirndls, bead ropes, chains,
drift between digs down streets whose names pre-date
the mills: Strawberry Bank, Shepherds Loan, Rose-
angle…that 'dear green place'. And all of the dole
kids drift really. And weren't we blessed to be
Supermac's kids – affluence fed welfare?
So lost out in private life, I should still
make something of this life, till shuffling off
immortal coil' – all's grist to self-accused
souls '…only connecting…loose threads like chains,
you have nothing to lose but…They shot that
Guy Burgess film in winter in Dundee –
City Square, Moscow. Half the snow was real.'

DUNDEE

Kenneth C. Steven

The water's oil. Out of the bladders of the sky
Low rain falls, smudging the brown tubas of tugs,
Boats skipping out on white curls of open sea.
This is Dundee. A slump on the banks of the Tay,
Left here by hammering industries, the jostle of progress.
Now unemployment's the biggest boss around.
Bored motorbikes wasp up streets, the televisions scream
Blue murder all day long. The odd lopsided seagull
Yelps Icelandic across the harbour, no fish dump
In shining waves across the piers. This place is dead.
Drive on, to the first rough edges of the north,
The fallow deer of the final hills.

DUNDEE
Dawn Wood

The Dichty Burn, his backbone
through Dronley above Baldovan –
mills along it and threats
of drowning cats, bad weans –

stretches past the seven arches
at Panmuirfield, to boil,
open-mouthed near Balmossie.
His horns, the Murroes and the Fithie,

Whitfield Burn, his tusk,
Dens Burn circles his Law Hill navel.
His claws, Lochee and the Scourin' Burn,
erupt at Balgay to grab

for the Pleiades ladies
and the pearl moon;
his wings are at the ready,
the Gorrie and the Gelly,

come the equinox, he'll rise;
trailing his tail feathers,
Liff and Fowlis,
from Benvie and the Swallow,

they'll ruffle and settle tomorrow.
A belly full of nine maidens
from Pitempton, says
the old wives' tale,

but stricken at Strathmartine.
Maybe a belly full of only rain
something of the city
to thunder in his mind

something of his mind,
tempted and draigled –
pours into brow and bone
of the city.

PROSPECT FROM BALGAY

George Maxwell

Oh! beauteous are thy sylvan slopes – Balgay;
    For fifty years they have familiar been,
    Yet, at this hour I love the peaceful scene
E'en more than ever in youth's primal day;
How placid lies the bosom of the Tay,
    Reflecting azure skies and hills of green,
    While spanning gulf which yawns the shire between
Is bridge gigantic, bearing iron way,
O'er which sweep trains, which potent steam obey
    In constant traffic to and from Dundee;
    My native town; which from Law's base we see
Extending Eastward far as eye can trace,
Its denizens full trebled, in the space
Of time embraced within my memory.

KING AND QUEEN OF THE LAW
Pippa Little

City of slopes and hills.
The Law, grandee of it all,
but Balgay, velveted with green
and Hilltown cobbles
I loved as much.

Built on the basalt plug
of a spent volcano, the only
Scottish city to face south,
you can see far and wide

widdershins to Fintry, the Sidlaws, the domino block
schemies, out to the sweep of the Tay where it accepts the sea,
even upriver towards Perth, the towers on suicide cliffs
those reclusive stories –

I've walked the bridge and back, and sailed on The Fifie
before that; I miss the lunge of my mother's car as
we hung between land and water for one endless moment
then down the ramp almost regained our gravity

but it's hills I remember, walking them with you:
that first bright dusk you told me
our only choice was to scramble the Law's steep side
so when breathless at the top I saw the road,

I should have known, but I didn't,
not for a long, long time.
Mill spinning left jute in your hair
I would pick out, rough and soft as terrier floss, blond
in your dark beard: your cut palms you sealed
with hot piss as the old men told you to, and I kissed them.

My days were dodging feral Alsatians across Kingsway East,
ruling through paragraphs with a crimson pen,
looking through layers of open-plan glass

for any real windows with real views – of the Law,
Cox's Stack, the Old Steeple, anywhere life
was always happening –

you get a kick even now from the sight of a hill,
wanting to drive up there, rather than stride it, though.
The city's so small in the frame of a car wing-mirror.
Always windy on the Law, no matter the season
and we're no longer king or queen, only the sum of
all those years small and intact now
as train carriages I see from this height
receding across the bridge, reflected in the water.

TAY BRIDGE
Elliot Rudie

All gone
    MacGonagall
Where your
    Tackety Boots
Walked pavements
    'Most terrible
To be seen.'

The cars race
    The diesel trains
To landfall
    By the green.

Taybridge, greybridge
    Blue all night,
Silver river cages
    On moon-iron sight.

Where drown
    Drop-hammer
Flame fell
    Off the night,
And train
    And carriages
Struck stormburst
    Iron down
Bridged height.

Blackness at nighttime
    Esplanade waiting,
Not the right time
    For Tay Bridge hating.

On Magdalen Green
    No-one is seen,
Nothing alive
    On Riverside Drive.

PORT SELDA
W. N. Herbert

I remember when all these fields were factories,
when an industry was the limitation beyond which
the city couldn't think. Before
our shorefronts needed to know
what their former yards had built
to fill in the information boards.
This was before the bomb, the bomb,
the modernist bomb,
the bomb that cleanses.

Picture a Heinkel, thrown into a himmelwarp
by passing over Bonnybridge in 1942,
emerging to continue its mission in the mid –
60s and blow Dundee, blow
all your cities backwards.

Wonderfully my grandfather, though dead,
is still on duty in the volunteer fire service,
and able to catch the first few incendiaries,
like women fainting at a dance, vomitting on
their heavy spangly dresses:
his helmet gleams like a pie-dish on the drainer.
But then the heavy-nippled storm begins.
Only the buildings of historic or
architectural interest are struck;
only the quarters of any character are hit.

The bomber is felled by an indignant bottle
cast from Lochee, where its casualties lie,
pants around their smoking ankles,
their budgies gargling their last
in the cracked uncacked-in toilet bowls.
A policeman like a column of oatmeal points
his shaking revolver at
the jute-coloured head of the survivor,
pulled from the harbour, who says,

'The question here is where to put the muzzle?
The stomach beckons, then the ear, the mouth.
Your indecision is built from endings:
it's built of evenings smoking out to sea
in a wake of oil and clocks and bobbing canisters;
it's built of absent records huddled in
your memory's implosive shelter;
it's built of everything that travels back
to the engine – the angel, the heart, the honey.

Through such compelling darknesses
its answer always comes:
"'What is looking for us in all these means?'"

SEAGATE
Raymond Falconer

Memory breaks its sleep
a spool unwinds,
someone pulls the thread
and cuts my skin.
Love lies bleeding
in a gazebo overlooking the Tay.
Wide, flat blue water.
Cold autumn sun flashes on a train.

Tay bridge gazebo disaster
nineteen seventy four.
Autumn morning in a coffee shop,
artistic words of Tayport
bounce awkwardly in the conversation
like sugar granules on the table,
mixing with the last person's coffee,
mixing with the last poet's ghostliness.

A snuffed candle smells
an old painting gets curled corners.
A protégé faked for use in and out
of focus hysterical romance has to be
reborn.

All I have to do is be shy with
my head wait for a fall,
spread my fingers on a desk
read the correct books.
Recollect the necessary friends
cross palms,
ditch self-pity and die on a proven
doorstep.

Waiting for a guide to tug my coat
the wind holds judgement
for me and the leaves upon
this road.
Headstrong wonder carved up or out of
ill fated confidence. Lacking other things
to do I scuff through the leaves.

In a coffee shop
tapping my heels under the table.
Outside, the Nethergate, almost as
it was
with the sun in just the right place.
I ought to cross the gap between old
friends and enemies with a typewriter
that has an O that sticks.
I lie awake at night though,
memorising the Tay.
No tricks.

NOCTURNE IN A DEAD STREET
Norrie Elder

Cats pad the flowering weedlands
their farflung mews purpling the silences
but nothing can storm the Great Silence
the unimaginable silence of the dead street.

Not drowning gutters disturb it
nor the rank evil seep of jagged rones;
the toppling chimneys, the crumbling slates
the dank striptease of paper, plaster,

slow as a scatter of broken orbits
still drift through the night of chronology.
Nothing to touch the determined silence;
old wounds, old bones,
obscurity.

THE BENCH
Anne Stevenson

Steep path to where the wheatfields' yellow
makes a plush gilt frame for the town.
A bench there – no back, but a view –
for lovers, dog-walkers, poets. Tired men
with sensational newspapers climb there, too.

HOME TOWN
Susan Sim

Dundee beats slow with a tired warm heart
Ricket-ridden buses shoogle tin-patched husks
Through arteries of streets, returning
Apathetic life-blood to bone-white fists of schemes.

Genial anachronism, turning out flat pockets
To line the sooty shells of warehouses
Sandblasting with borrowed sixpences
Strongboxes resonant with barefoot ghosts.

Dundee beats slow with a tired warm heart
Muffled like the clapper in an old bell.

CRAIGIE PARK
G.F. Dutton

All these leaves
scarlet and crimson
on the grass

wet grass; Berberis,
Cotoneaster, the more talented
hybrid rowans, have shed them

it being autumn
and the time
to lay things down.

And to light up
doorways, windows
early, draw across

curtains brightly
at every room;
so many colours

springing about us, a necklace, a nightly
clasping of welcome
as we reach home.

Street after street, and almost too late.
A ring round the heart
fastening tight

as leaves go out
and the grass gutters
to a dark centre without stars.

NIGHT GULLS, DUNDEE
Jim Stewart

Given that I know there are no ghosts
and that the only phantom is my fear,
what would cause this shudder isn't clear
as the night gulls glide through Dundee in their hosts.

Perhaps, unusually, it's that they'd scream
but now are quiet, apparent in a dark
I didn't know contained them – stark
and white, and half remembered from a dream.

The night is theirs not mine. This vacant street
walked by all the generations dead
is flown by birds which having lost their dread,
rip the precinct's bin bags for their meat.

Perhaps they are the wraiths of gulls long gone
whose suddenness is what gives mild alarm,
focused and impervious to harm,
stomachs empty hours before the dawn.

Their silent spirits close to mine, I can't
think what made me start like this. They fly
in search of lost abandoned food; and I
haunt their streets, untimely, revenant.

DUNDEE
Colette Bryce

Take the east coast line,
the spine,
leave London, Peterborough, York, Newcastle upon Tyne
behind,
relax…unwind.
If you sway through the carriages to coach 9
you can dine,
chill with a glass of wine,
see Edinburgh blaze in the late sunshine.

Continue north. Let's say
An hour more, the scenic, coastal way,
*Aberdour, Burntisland…*pass *Kirkcaldy;*

then farmland – fields of rolled-up hay
like some golden board-game,
    stalled, awaiting play –

Until the train slows in reverence
    as you cross the bridge where the river swells to the estuary,
the Firth of Tay.

That's where you'll find me, these days.

FAREWELL LOCHEE BRIG
David Phillips

It kent the lang-drahn grumblin'
O' troop trains' heavy load
An' echoed tae the marchin'
O' battalions on the road ...

Cerriage windies, brightened
Wi' bairnies' wavin' hands,
Awa' for country picnic
Or joyous day on sands.

It kent the coughin' clatter
O' steam cars belchin' through,
An' sparks fae hooves hae marked
The jeit-kerts passin' slow.

'Twas Lochee fowk's great symbol
That somehow they were free;
A sign o' independence
Fae a'-devourin' Dundee.

Well, for many a year now
It hasna made the news ...
Now a nostalgic gap,
Wan mair place less for doos ...

But though bairns grou' withoot it
WE'LL aye see it in mind's ee,
A phantom brig aye wi' us
As the Frontier o' Lochee.

SEPTEMBER FIRES
Margaret Gillies Brown

Late evening and a light wind
Sends farmers burning straw in harvest fields.
From where I stand, warm in an anorak,
I see dancing coronas, flickering gold,
Releasing smoke, the colour of sunsets,
To drift and rise into
An egg shell sky.

There, beneath the hills,
A Castle flares in light – is gone!
Towards the east, the three-pronged dovecot,
Centuries old, stands out in black relief.
Fires expand space, an optical illusion
But viewed from higher ground
It must look as though
The cities of the plains are burning.

Beside me, the apple orchard
Holds in her dark green breath –
Daring the long sierras of fire
To come much closer;
The top of the oak tree glows with light
And farmhouse chimneys blush and pale again.

Tonight, fantastic movement, flame-red energy,
Tomorrow, stillness and the black scorched earth
Cleaned and ready to take new seed
In whose dark cells …

Lie the germ
Of their own destruction.

MAGGIE'S CENTRE
Forbes Browne

A roof made of gulls' wings
hovering over the curved, protective wall
of a vast, white broch;
a slim, stainless steel smokestack
soaring to the sky from a wood stove –
warm heart of the building.

A shining array of glass and pale timber,
walls of colour, tapestries, paintings, books;
a wooden walkway striding towards
forest, river and distant hills.

DRAWING THE CURTAIN
Val Warner

Drawing the curtain on the day,
the dun and mist, the white

…I turn in on my dusty room,
a litter of living and newspapers.

At dusk, it's hard not to be

yearning after skeletal trees, the Tay
unwound to sea with drowned
dreams…lengthening days. Away
from the front

of this block, you don't hear the thunder
of the traffic, back-firing
past on the road to Dundee,
past the city's Western Cemetery.

Greys and dun compose the day,
that would stick in my mind
and in the sinking light is
gilded in passing

like the odd purple patch
of heather,
and beyond the pale

flowers o' the forest
at the iron gate
at the necropolis, just
down the road.

MOUNT PLEASANT

J. B. Salmond

Search in the sunshine or seach in the rain,
You'll never find candles in Candle Lane;
Or wander a year in Sugar House Wynd
And never a spoonful of sugar you'll find;
Take your basket to Strawberry Bank in the sun
And of strawberries you will get never a one.

But up in Mount Pleasant one morning in June
I saw an old chap in his carpet-shoon
Take his ease at the top of an old outside stair,
While the sun glinted down on the old silvered hair,
And he puffed at his pipe in an old-fashioned way,
And he said to me 'Ay, but it's pleasant the day !'

'Where have you been for your blossoming load?'
'I've been for my lillies to Lilybank Road,'
'Where is the garden with flowers so sweet?'
'In an old woman's barrow. She comes to the street.
Her cheeks are like roses, her eyes all sky-clear,
And she asked God to bless me, and called me 'my dear.'
And what more, good sir, can the best garden do
Than call down the blessing of God upon you?'

ON THE CITY OF DUNDEE

Alexander Nicol

Near where the Tay joins with the ocean wide,
Dundee's fair harbour stands on its north side,
Where ships of burden safely can repose,
While billows rise, and loudest tempest blows.

The ancient city, fam'd for arms and arts,
Parent of many that have shown their parts,
Nothing inferior to the world abroad;
Such to this city is the gift of God.

Dundee is peopled with a prudent race
Of wealthy traders, that enrich the place;
To strangers kind, and hospitably good,
With manly virtues almost all endu'd.

Where ancient buildings were by time defac'd,
More spacious new ones in their rooms are plac'd:
An ancient steeple rears its head on high,
O'erlooks the town, and penetrates the sky;
Strangers admire, when it afar they spy.
A new town-house, much like a palace fair;
None of its kind can with it once compare:

Their care and prudence did of old provide
An hospital for those that are decay'd;
Two ancient churches, decently decor'd
With all utensils necessar well stor'd.

Accommodations they have many now,
Which their ancestors ne'er so much as knew:
The water-works that turneth as they please
To quench with speed the flames devouring bleeze;
Lamps in the streets that give a splendid light,
Whereby we walk safe in the darkest night;
An ancient spring, whose streams long useless stray'd,
In leaden conduits now are all convey'd

From street to street, the cities multitude
By them's supplied with water fresh and good.

But ancient things commodious and great,
Buildings and wealth, these ne'er secure the state.
Where's Babel, Troy, and fam'd Jerusalem?
There's scarce a vestige to be found of them;
For pride and lust, and wretch'd idolatry,
Bloodshed and rapine, and proud tyranny,
Long since have made them in oblivion ly.

But, lo! Dundee's fam'd citizens have been,
Thro' ages past, for virtuous actions keen:
Their fervent zeal for pure religion shin'd,
And left the rest of Scotland far behind,
And with the work of reformation join'd.

Here virgin beauties, with such lustre shine,
That ev'ry charm about them seems divine:
Here virtuous matrons, chastly fix'd in love,
That to their husbands helps and comforts prove:
Here men of learning, honour and renown,
In ev'ry age, have grac'd this ancient town:

Hail, ancient city! citizens, all hail!
May ne'er your grandeur, wealth and honours fail!
Thy trade still prosper both by sea and land!
What-e'er you wish be still at your command!
Let your religion flourish still in thee,
Thy greatest glory since thou wast Dundee!

3
THE TIMES

EXCERPT FROM 'THE WALLACE'
Blind Harry

Upon a day to Dundé he was send;
Of cruelnes full litill thai him kend.
The constable, a felloun man of wer,
That to the Scottis he did full mekill der,
Selbye he hecht, dispitfull and owtrage.
A sone he had ner twenty yer of age,
Into the toun he usyt evirilk day.
Thre men or four thar went with him to play,
A hely schrew, wanton in his entent.
Wallace he saw and towart him he went.
Likle he was, rycht byge and weyle beseyne
Intill a gyde of gudly ganand greyne.
He callyt on hym and said, 'Thow Scot, abyde.
Quha devill thee grathis in so gay a gyde?
Ane Ersche mantill it war thi kynd to wer,
A Scottis thewtill undyr thi belt to ber,
Rouch rewlyngis apon thi harlot fete.
Gyff me thi knyff. Quhat dois thi ger so mete?'
Till him he yeid his knyff to tak him fra.
Fast by the collar Wallace couth him ta.
Undyr his hand the knyff he bradit owt,
For all his men that semblyt him about,
Bot help himselff he wyst of no remede.
Without reskew he stekyt him to dede.
The squier fell, of him thar was na mar.
His men folowid on Wallace wondir sar.
The pres was thik and cummirit thaim full fast.
Wallace was spedy and gretlye als agast,
The bludy knyff bar drawin in his hand;
He sparyt nane that he befor him fand.
He knew the hous his eyme had lugit in;
Thedir he fled for owt he mycht nocht wyn.
The gude wyff than within the clos saw he
And 'help!' he cryit, 'for him that deit on Tre.
The yong captane has fallyn with me at stryff.'
In at the dure he went with this gud wiff.

A roussat goun of hir awn scho him gaif
Apon his weyd at coveryt all the layff,
A soudly courche our hed and nek leit fall;
A wovyn quhyt hatt scho brassit on withall,
For thai suld nocht lang tary at that in;
Gaiff him a rok, syn set him doun to spyn.
The Sothroun socht quhar Wallace was in drede.
Thai wyst nocht weylle at quhat gett he in yeide.
In that same hous thai socht him beselye
Bot he sat still and span full conandly,
As of his tym, for he nocht leryt lang.
Thai left him swa and furth thar gait can gang
With hevy cheyr and sorowfull in thocht.
Mar witt of him as than get couth thai nocht...

GOD SEND EVERIE PREIST ANE WYFE

John Wedderburn

God send everie Preist ane wyfe,
And everie Nunne ane man,
That thay mycht leue that haly lyfe
As first the Kirk began.

Sanct Peter, quhome nane can reprufe,
His lyfe in Mariage led :
All guide Preistis, quhome God did lufe,
Thair maryit wyffis had.

Greit causis than, I grant, had thay
Fra wyffis to refraine :
Bot greiter causis haif thay may,
Now wyffis to wed againe.

For than suld nocht sa mony hure
Be up and downe this land :
Nor yit sa mony beggeris pure,
In Kirk and mercat stand.

And nocht sa mekle bastard seid,
Throw out this cuntrie sawin :
Nor gude men uncouth fry suld feid,
And all the suith war knawin.

Sen Christis law, and commoun law,
And Doctouris will admit,
That Preistis in that yock suld draw,
Quha dar say contrair it ?

FOONDRY LANE
Mary Brooksbank

There's a Juter and a Battener
    Sailing up the Tay,
And a' the wives in Foondry Lane
    Are singing blithe the day.
There'll be pennies for the bairnies,
    A pint for Jock and Tam,
Money for the picters,
    The auld fowk get a dram.

We'll gie the secks the go by,
    We canna sew and eat,
And fivepence for twenty-five
    Will no buy muckle meat.
We'll hae steak and ingins frying,
    Lift oor claes a' oot the pawn,
We'll gaither wulks and boil them
    In a corn beef can.

OMEGA

James Hall Thomson

On a clear night from a cold North Street Hall
you could hear the heat of a rehearsal's ball.
A precise yet quivering New Orleansian horn
leading us through our marches and blues
while a pianist with a penchant for the 13-bar form
and for losing the middle-eight part of a theme
would vocalize raucously TIRALEE TIRALAA.
And no worse for a fungus that grew round his bend
the trombonist burped his bass counterpoint
and the drummer accelerated as the number advanced
and Buddy de Wardrobe with amplified bass
slapped a two-beat excuse for the smile on his face.

The rhythm would bend our uncertainties whole –
propel the group forward with assets of fault –
our fractions all flattened as well as our fifths.
Bourbon Street, Saratoga, The Jazz Band Ball,
Whether Delta, Ellington, Chicago drawl –
We tried it all and we did it all
From Lonely Hearts Club to Masonic Hall –
From Art Revels romp to Riverboat shout.

You could hear the heat from a rehearsal's ball
any clear night from the cold North Street Hall.

SLANT
Pippa Little

I love the Howff, those gravestones soft as horses,
the Seagate, Perth Road's long sweep
in blue evening, lamps coming on
across the railway lines:
each adds to the brew, well-stirred.

When I lived in Dundee they were pulling it down.
Tenements foundered on red rubble cliffs,
washing greens, out-houses, all gone.
The Victorians were just as eager,
atomising Butchers Row
the fish and butter markets' medieval huddle
to raise civic swaggers of Institutions
for imbecile and idiot children,
the respectable blind –

I might come across my grandfather on the High Street,
walk through an architrave where his office used to be
or pass through him so I make us sweat.
I know how any musty, unwritten-on
black and white photograph feels:
look slant, you'll see us,
and through all the layers between the light
we'll see you.

THE TAY BRIDGE DISASTER
William McGonagall

Beautiful Railway Bridge of the Silv'ry Tay!
Alas! I am very sorry to say
That ninety lives have been taken away
On the last Sabbath day of 1879,
Which will be remember'd for a very long time.

'Twas about seven o'clock at night,
And the wind it blew with all its might,
And the rain came pouring down,
And the dark clouds seem'd to frown,
And the Demon of the air seem'd to say —
'I'll blow down the Bridge of Tay.'

When the train left Edinburgh
The passengers' hearts were light and felt no sorrow,
But Boreas blew a terrific gale,
Which made their hearts for to quail,
And many of the passengers with fear did say —
'I hope God will send us safe across the Bridge of Tay.'

But when the train came near to Wormit Bay,
Boreas he did loud and angry bray,
And shook the central girders of the Bridge of Tay
On the last Sabbath day of 1879,
Which will be remember'd for a very long time.

So the train sped on with all its might,
And Bonnie Dundee soon hove in sight,
And the passengers' hearts felt light,
Thinking they would enjoy themselves on the New Year,
With their friends at home they lov'd most dear,
And wish them all a happy New Year.

So the train mov'd slowly along the Bridge of Tay,
Until it was about midway,
Then the central girders with a crash gave way,

And down went the train and passengers into the Tay!
The Storm Fiend did loudly bray,
Because ninety lives had been taken away,
On the last Sabbath day of 1879,
Which will be remember'd for a very long time.

As soon as the catastrophe came to be known
The alarm from mouth to mouth was blown,
And the cry rang out all o'er the town,
Good Heavens! the Tay Bridge is blown down,
And a passenger train from Edinburgh,
Which fill'd all the peoples hearts with sorrow,
And made them for to turn pale,
Because none of the passengers were sav'd to tell the tale
How the disaster happen'd on the last Sabbath day of 1879,
Which will be remember'd for a very long time.

It must have been an awful sight,
To witness in the dusky moonlight,
While the Storm Fiend did laugh, and angry did bray,
Along the Railway Bridge of the Silv'ry Tay,
Oh! ill-fated Bridge of the Silv'ry Tay,
I must now conclude my lay
By telling the world fearlessly without the least dismay,
That your central girders would not have given way,
At least many sensible men do say,
Had they been supported on each side with buttresses,
At least many sensible men confesses,
For the stronger we our houses do build,
The less chance we have of being killed.

OCCASION
G.F. Dutton

down what are called streets
the whole corsage of pity
floats by, laughing, after the storm.
the delicate confetti
vanishes into a drain.

doors bang, gears complain,
and after the tyres' disturbance
journeys begin again.
tall houses, with sealed lips,
billow a little, and are gone.

I turn to you sitting beside me
breathless and close, but
you have leant back in your white veil
and our eyes are shut.

THE FIFIE
Joseph Lee

"'There was a ship,' quoth he."—The Rime of the Ancyent Marinere.

O' a' the ships that sail the sea,
The strangest far bekenn'd to me,
Is that fair craft—an' nane but she —
    Sae justly famed,
That plies 'twixt Newport an' Dundee —
    The 'Fifie' named.

I've seen a wheen o' curious craft —
Dhow', dahabeah, 'dola, raft,
O' various build an' different draught —
    Yea, mony a barque,
But never heard o' thing sae daft
    Since Noah's ark.

'Twad tax a landsman to discern
Whare lies her stem an' whare her stern;
A thing whilk I could never learn,
    Tho' sair I've tried —
It's said that she can tak' a turn
    Wi' her broadside.

Her speed is onything but slow —
Sometimes six knots an hour or so;
The grass has little time to grow,
    Things fairly hum —
Yet twa young men no lang ago
    Got out an' swum!

The folks upon the upper deck
Keep pacing on wi' ne'er a check,
As they were walking neck-an'-neck
    For wage or wagers,
Wi' airs an' gestures mony feck —
    Just like Drum-Majors.

Behold the 'Fifie' stem the Tay,
And score o' Newport sancts convey
To hear some city parson pray
    In church on Sunday —

A miracle indeed if they
    Arrive by Monday!

For dangers lie on every hand,
An' if she shudna chance to strand
Upon some hidden bank o' sand,
    Then a'most certain,
A fog fa's doon an' hides the land
    Wi' sable curtain.

An' when there's naething else the matter,
Be sure there's no enough o' water
Alangside o' the pier to lat her —
    The folks gang wud,
Ashore when they hae got to splatter
    Thro' a' the mud!

Fareweel auld 'Fifie', gang your ways,
An' heedna what my mad muse says,
Some ither day she'll sing thy praise
    Wi' pen an' tongue,
An' loud panegyrics will raise
    To Captain Young!

MUSEUM PHOTOGRAPH BROUGHTY FERRY
Stan Smith

Corner of Gray Street and King Street,
July 8th, 1893. Never again
will it be just like this.

In the doorway of the corner store
a man in an apron white to his shins
stares at the camera with as much intent
as if he must outface it, to survive.

I have replaced the lens: he stares at me.

Along King Street a woman paused with a high pram
frowns as if she still has somewhere to go;
the children playing in Gray Street which recedes
from my not quite decent gaze
spy off the edge the uncharted
regions where lurk monsters.

A photo of my grandfather, slight,
wiry and bewhiskered whitely,
that I cannot trace, outside his ironmonger's
among metal buckets, teacups and the rest,
is not so fraught with perils as this print.
He died when I was four, but is familiar
as my own shadow on the same street, moving
forever in the light of anecdote.

No legends hold this corner for my loss.
The moustachioed patriarch, first of his line;
these dubious children, the lady with the pram,
long dead in the possession of a street
which knows no bounds.

Souls lost in a traffic intimately theirs.
No family albums fix the cracking plate.
I am cast out. Before and after time
they reside. I pass, and
another gaze succeeds me.

NINEWELLS

J. B. Salmond

A tinker cam' tae the Ninewells,
    An' a thirsty man was he.
But the parson needed a well for himsel',
    An' the lawyer needed three;
An' twa were set aside for the Laird
    An' twa for his Lady fair;
An' the village waa' at the Ninth well,
    So there was na' ane tae spare.
Then the tinker loofed his hands to the rain,
But he ne'er took the Ninewells road again.

THI LA' HILL

Gary Robertson

Yiv witnessed thi birth o meh hame toon Dundee
Yiv seen ir prosper – an expand fae thi sea
Come tell me La' Hill o ir characters an sights
Yiv musta seen it ah, fae yir towerin heights
Wit wiz it like wen Edwardz army marched in?
Plunderin wir toon an murderin wir kin
Ye musta seen Wallace wi thi chib in eez hand
Gub thi Constable's son an tak thi patriot stand

Yiv seen thi Aald Steeple buhlt up brick-beh-brick
A safe haven fir wurshippirz scared o Aald Nick
Mind it wizna that safe wen General Monck's mob arrehvd
Thi pillage an thi slaughter left scant few alehv
Yiv musta asked yirsel often, 'Why di men hae ti fight?'
Az ye waatched Dundeez sons, march or sail oot ih sight
Thir blood soaked in thi soil, in landz far fae heer
Eh, yood see, an stull see, thir puir mithirz grievin tearz

Ye widda seen mind, thi growth o thi Industrial Revolution
An then again, mibbee no, wi ah thi smog an pollution
Thi massiz swaarmin in, through thi factaryz an thi millz
Thi jute, jam an journalism an ah thi shipbuhldirz skillz
Whalers like thi Baleena, buhlt right heer in oor docks
Thi Discovery an Terra Nova, buhlt ti tak arctic knocks
Eh, thay tall masts ye saw venture oot on thi Tay
Kerried Shackleton an Scott, on thir Antarctic way

UNTITLED
Syd Scroggie

Look out for new employment,
You men of NCR
Unhitch your creaking wagon
From Nelson's waning star.
It's shrinking weeks of wages
And pay-offs from now on
Till every man's redundant
And every job is gone.

Time was we marched victorious
And vanquished every foe
And fat production figures
Maintained an even flow;
In business, shop and office,
Exchange and public bar
Every cash transaction
Was labeled NCR

But now the plant is empty
And in the silent street
You only hear the echo
Of Nelson's old, tired feet.
Where are his vast pretensions?
They weren't worth a rap.
For Swedes and Japs and Germans
Have wiped us off the map.

Look out for new employment
You men of NCR
Unhitch your creaking wagon
From Nelson's waning star.
And if you should fall idle
We've got good news for you;
They are taking in the Caird Hall
And extending the Burroo.

THE LIFE CYCLE OF THE BARRACUDA
Judith Taylor

In the mid-Seventies, it was The Place To Be.
At least, there wasn't anyplace else much
in that old industrial drinking town.
I was too young for its glory days.
The bus home from the shops went past its door
and I would stare into its concrete-fanged, shadowy maw
and wonder what went on there.
I remember most the adverts in the paper
with the letters of its name all
sharpened, finned; shaped in imitation.

But by the time I got there it was too late:
the Eighties. By then it was the *Coconut Grove*,
defanged, and crammed with fake trees
like a nightmare based on a *Wham* song.
The floor was full of girls in white and stilettos
and the bar, of saddening older men who hated dancing
drinking up their courage.
The DJ played the same two or three twelve-inch mixes
back to back all night. And God, the desperation.

Even I got chatted up
– by a golf knitwear salesman
passing through en route to St Andrews.
We laughed about it afterwards in the taxi, but
a sad time.

By the Nineties it was property
like everything else in the Nineties.
Quick changes of name and ownership;
big plans that never came to pass: nobody was surprised much
when it burned down, and the paper
carried rumours of extradition warrants.
Then, I suspect, an argument over who the ruins belonged to:
after the site was cleared, it saw the decade out as a car park,
nothing but dust and buddleia

in the place that used to be The Place.
The last time I went round that way it was gone
under a supermarket.

Early in the evening, then: the time the city becomes deep
and blue, and seems mysterious
as an ocean, still. And around the place it was,
the former churches, former garages, former mills swam, all
sharpened, neon-finned; shaped in imitation.

LIFEBOAT DISASTER, APRIL 1960

William Montgomerie

To James Coull, coxswain

> *Tween the Isle of May*
> *and the Links o Tay*
> *mony a ship's been cast awa*

Folkrhyme

Storm
from the North Sea's December
over St Andrews Bay
over eider muirs of Fife
and two miles of white estuary
north against this shore

Sand sifts out of the south
soft as blown mist over a muir
in headlights of motorcars
from the beach where
dunlins twittered all night
a flurry of fine sand
on the esplanade
a scurry of sand in a lane
drifting for a night
a day
and half a night
over roads
over pavements
over parapets into gardens

Sand and fine rain find
warped wood and weathering stone
finger a salt-rusted catch
find a draught in the window frame
spill an hourglass on the floor
All this second night

the wind drops slated into gardens
bends steel radio masts at the chimney
smashes their teeth on the slates

All night
a mad gate beats against a broken lock

We lean back
on the black wind
watch our footprints by the lamp
drift away in a mist of sand
and listen

Hours are blown with the rain
three oystercatchers flee over the wet slates
calling

A buoy flashes
red
in the fairway
to the four-mile faraway city
the Horseshoe counting
four-and-a dark seconds
flashes silver

Darkness the dragon has eaten the Lady
and a sea-mist the lightship
In the fairway by the Gaa Sands
black night the cormorant
shakes the third light
and swallows it
South-east by the Fife skerries
the North Carr rocks her crew
looses the cat-clawing anchor
drifts
eight men and a light
drifts and holds
on the last anchor

The first maroon knocks loudly
once
on the wet shutters of heaven
drops a green firefly
They wake in cottage bedrooms
open the curtain
watch the sky

Unchained
our lifeboat is loosed
to the indifferent sea
where storms
forecast from cottage radios
meet the timetable tide
beginning its slow ivy crawl
up wormcast beaches
up posts and harbour walls
washing the glass hands of barnacles

The lifeboat rolls
rises
dips past the pilot's pier
(where in other midnights
the silver wash under the jetty
flickers on the black cutter's hull
going up
going down
in the lift of the tides)
past the swimming club
and the castle
(whose cannon once guarded the narrows
whose war rockets like two hands
ripped the canvas of the sky)

Forty horsepower under the floorboards
galloping
beat under the bootsoles of the crew
The coxswain defines his straight line
through the rain curtains and the mist drifting

102

and a lost gull silver in the searchlight
The coastguards watch from the two shores
the short waves talk to one another

'Jist passin the Abertay lightship'

'Jist approachin positions o the Middle Buoys'

'The North Carr Lightship has fired
a white flare
Can you see the flare?
an gie me yer position!'

'Aye we see that ane
but we're no clear yet'

All night the short waves talk
to the silent dark
but the dark comprehends it not
nor the silence
round the last corner of time
for beyond the bar over the Gaa Sands
the Mona has rolled over her crew
Ronald Grant Coxswain and his seven
holding them under water
like a swan a duck
or a mother smothering her bairns
rolling over them
and lies mastless
a coffin on the beach
with seven drowned men
and a man missing

The plaque on the boathouse wall honours them

*   *   *   *   *   *

The weathercock on the kirk steeple
swings on the wind blowing

from the North Sea
from Fife
(the beggar's cloak with the fringe of gold)
from Atlantis and
in lee of the cold
five men turn in time with
the tail of the gold cock
All day by the lifeboat shed
they loiter by the steps
down to the pebbled beach
or on the road by the dead men's plaque
or on the beach sand
out of the west wind

Here is the sump for whalers' tales told
in the Ship Inn bar
sailors' tales
war tales I shall tell elsewhere
lifeboat tales and
scraps of newspaper
blown down Fort Street to the boathouse

'Whit wey wiz the boathook lashed tae the wheel?
an the engineroom hatch open
that midnicht tae wind and watter?
an the droont mechanic halfwey tae the engine?'

They quiz the Inquisitor's verdict
the lifeboat Mona guilty of witchcraft
having said nothing in her own defence
handed over to the secular arm for burning
in another place to avoid local disturbance

I have stood by your Coxswain James Coull
at your wheel
your two hands relaxed
your knees lax
would tense like a boxer's
when the feint and the knock-out come together

when the feint and the knock-out were two waves
almost together
countered on the wheel
by your hair-trigger fingertips
ere your brain knew
a skill coiled and oiled
in hands and arms
in thirty storms in twenty five years
that brought a hundred lives and more
ashore
to hot tea and buns in the Kirk hall
a skill not to be learned in five weeks

I am remembering a dozen heroes who harried Hell
beginning with Orpheus who went to Hades
to bring back Eurydice his wife
(one life)
And failed

You
Coxswain
went thirty times into chaos
and came back with a hundred lives

From Theseus in the Labyrinth
killing the Minotaur
bull-headed son of the white bull
and nymphomaniac Pasiphae
I turn to
a live black bull
an earthquake shaking the ground
to Ordoñez the bullfighter
between two horns nagging Death
killing
with a surgeon's skill between the shoulder blades
and from him to this quiet man
facing the bull of the sea bellowing against the land
from the cold labyrinth of waves and wind
where underfoot moves in three dimensions

from the myths of death
to the truth of death
from death to life
and a saviour of life

The five men by the lifeboat station
have watched you pass along Fisher Street
like Dante from Hell
scorched by your lifeboat burning

ENTERING DUNDEE
Walter Thornbury

Shouting 'Goring!' slashing, roaring,
   Singing, swearing, musket flaring, colours blowing free,
On a day in pleasant May, never minding right of way,
   Never stopping shot to pay,
     Merry rode the troopers into fair Dundee.

Sparrow-shooting, crying, hooting,
   Tossing, prancing, pennon dancing, through the window see –
Clashing scabbard, not a laggard, spurring fast from lea and haggard,
   Shaking every noisy scabbard,
     Merry rode the troopers into fair Dundee.

DUNDEE DAY TRIPPER
Lydia Robb

The ither day
a tramcar cam
rummlin doun
the Nethergate
o ma memory.

It stoaped outside
the Greens Playhoose,
whaur an auld film
flickert backarties
in black an white.

Ootbye, a puckle
camsteerie council chiels
got cairried awa wi themsels,
yoked up a Trojan cuddy
an ploud throu the Overgate.

Craws cowpit
fae the corbie stanes
an the auld toun
turnt tae stour,
happit harns in hodden grey.

The bummer gaed.
Words skellt fae
The mou o the *Courier* biggin;
Fell on deif lugs.

At the terminus
ma lines got raivelt,
laivin ma thochts
hingin like the washin
on the plettie.

GENERAL GRANT'S VISIT TO DUNDEE
Michael Marra

When U.S. Grant paid a visit to my home town
They spruced it up with a lick of paint
And they showed him round
Two bands played in fierce competition
As the rain cam down
And the General said, 'What a mighty long bridge to such
A mighty little ole town.'

A man called Walsh hung from a window
With the stars and stripes
And the Orphan Boys sang, 'Allouette'
Sweetness and light
But as they sang the fire bell rang
And they ran for their lives
'What well trained little orphans,
Such a precious little song,' said the General's wife.

A carriage was called to the Magdalen Green
Before the darkness fell
With a short stop over for the ladies' convenience
At the Royal Hotel
And the General frowned
Through the last of the speeches
Though he took it well
'Not a pretty little band stand, or a lovely little steeple
What charming little houses
And such cheerful little people
But what a mighty long bridge
To such a mighty little ole town.'

TEXTILE TOUN

Kate Armstrong

Time the warp an skill the wab
an the shuttle the will tae mak a thing,
an the folk are threids an thrums, Jimmy,
the people threids an thrums.

See thon hole in Victoria Road;
hear the airth-movers rair!
Sune we'll drive on a brand new bypass,
a tunnel ablow the road, progress,
auld roads gone, shift the traffic on,
Mair is better is mair.

The young men dance in the concrete pit, wi a dream
o a clean shirt an a pint or twa for the stoor.
The guff o auld airth hings in their hair.

A rock seam seips dawn-sky-coloured mudstane, silvery slack
as herrin spilled frae the creel. No muckle wark
tae tamp it doon wi cement an a mile of steel.

The auld men staund at hame wi the dirdum,
clean hauns rest on the fence.
Their toun hoasted through a hundred years o jute.
Sand-bags, carpets, wallboard, aa' thing;
women hame late, barkit, weary;
an it's twa-three threids tae a weaver's knot,
an the Dundee weavers winna be forgot,
an they watch the new men rax in the pit
an they watch street threadin under street.
Dust birls up, blue denims whiten,
buits graw grey, bricht biceps tighten –
Jimmy, see's that pipe!
The mixers spew an the sweat wins through
an the levels set an rise. The airms that grip
the heckle an the grab are grist an mill;
a patch is darned in the city's twill, Jimmy,

raivellt, unraivellt
an the auld, thrawn, shiny rickle o mudstane
bricht an strange as yesterday's skill
trickles awa tae nothin, a crumb
in the gullet sune sweiled doon.
Bury it deep, Jimmy, time tae get on.

JUTE MILL SANG
Ellie McDonald

Baxters Upper Dens Mill, a hauf mile roun
o muckle stane waas an iron yetts.
The bummers quaet this lang while syne.
Nae siller nou in jute an niver wis
fur them that wrocht twal hours a day,
but gied a creshy linin tae the bosses' pouch
an biggit railroads hauf across America.

Ilka day, ilka day, ilka day, the hemmers
ding doun the waas o Baxters Upper Dens.
Naebody kens whit's tae be pitten in its place,
naebody greets for its demise.
An stour blaws frae the houkit out wame o't
sclairtan the cars an buses that birl awaa
tae concrete fields o spacelessness.

THE COFFIN MILL
James Adams

Before the big bang
well-tuned frames crooned
clacking songs. Bobbin
barrows raced clouded walkways,
calloused hands clocked
in from earlybird to starshift
Overloud noises weaned
sign languages suitable
for survival. Well-known
ghosts shambled through steerage,
cloth cap camaraderie
compensated for threatened
lifespans wrapped in coughs.

STRIKE SANG
Mary Brooksbank

We are out for higher wages,
    As we have a right to do,
And we'll never be content,
    Till we get oor ten per cent,
For we have a right to live
    As well as you.

DUNDEE JUTE MILL,
TURN OF THE CENTURY
Hugh McMillan

They stand crucified by loom ribs and spindles,
these hemp women made from shadow,
with their skull heads doubled over machines
that worked, but not for them.
They present their misery unabashed,
unwilling to hide it,
unable to conjure, for a shutter second, smiles.

In the foreground there is a youth.
He is small
(The nearest women are bending to his height)
but there is more than a hint of swagger
in the watch chain,
the slightly bending knee,
the hand laid proprietorially on a spool of cloth.
He is a golden boy:
he shines even in this glory of sepia.

It is the way the world is:
and you know the women will die
near the looms,
their certainties the more enduring,
and that the boy's chest will be torn
by machine guns,
all the puff and pride blown to smoke forever.
He will not live to see the skeleton of his mill
or hear the women, weeping still.

THE GLORY HAS DEPARTED (EXCERPT)
(After Walt Whitman)

James Geddes

This is what we have come to
    Here in the year of our Lord eighteen hundred and eighty-
eight;
This is the effect of coquetting with dignitaries;
This is the result of the Education Acts;
This is the sum total of the general diffusion of culture and the
spread of knowledge among the people.
Hitherto we have arrived —
Here where we are studying the beautiful only in connection with
the useful and the practical;
Here where we are bent on abrogating the merely ornamental;
Here where we are mediating the abolition of perpetual pensions
and the reform of the House of Lords;
Here when real men, when persons of genuine worth, refuse titles
— won't have them on any account:
Yes, this is where we are —
Dundee has applied for the title of City, and got it.

JIMMY REID'S
Gary Robertson

Afore navvies worked like navvies,
an buhlt thi La' Hill up
afore Thomas Bouch designed eez bridge,
wile pished in a Dundee pub
wen Betty White wiz stull a bairn,
an ir fruit shops wurna plantid
afore thi intriduction o thi cundee,
afore thi skeem fowk raved an rantid
wen Desperate Dan couldna pick a fuhl luggie,
well afore eez muscles hid grown
afore Dennis thi Menace wiz a menace,
afore thie Hackie or Shipirdz Loan
eh, afore ah them thir wiz Jimmy Reid's,
sellin anything, ivreehing an a'hin
in thid flock beh thi coachload,
an canoe doon thi Burnie fae Linla'hin

Queuein fae Samualz ti thi Seagate,
jist ti grab a wee bargain or twa
like a car-boot sale in a phone box,
thi puntirz stowed thi place wa ti bliddee wa
Showaddywaddy mirriz an flooree nylon sheetz,
puhly cases an Elvis Presley clocks
sna shakerz, Snoopy waatchiz, tea-strainirz —
an replica Mary Slessor frocks
mind, it musta been aboot 72,
wen sum o Jimmy's stock went fir a song
thi cheese-cloth-jute-lined-Terry-towellin trunks,
an eez world faimiss clingfuhlm thongz
quiltz, hobnail baitz an Black Waatch kiltz —
an hade-squares fir sweet aald grannayz
an thi fragrances 'Midnight at thi Dichty' —
'Oxtir Ming' an 'Essence o' thi Swaanayz'

Shop tull ye drap at Reid's Shangri-La,
tea-cosies fehv fir a quid
bric-a-brac an brac-a-bric dockies —
thingys, doofirz an hoojee-ka-pivz
wahr else in thi toon supplehz sich choice?
certainly no yir la-dee-da designer skwaad
thay couldna sell keech ti a gairdnir —
wah cares fir thir 'must-hae' fadz
fae boonsee baz ti fake chocolate tea potz,
shoartbrade an langbrade an ah
thi complete Daphne Broon range o lingerie,
an Alvin Stardust phoataze hingin on thi wah
plehty polish, Wulliam Wahliss t-shirtz,
an manualz on how ti play thi wahshie
puncture repair outfitz fir Penny-farthin bikes,
an toupeez in thi style o Shirley Bassey

Ower thi yearz Jimmy's selt thi bliddee lot —
an litz hope, thi story kerries on
az pure Dundee az thi peh ee iz —
a real legendary retail icon
thi opposition canna fathom it oot —
thi jist huvna got a Daniel Doo
David keepz beltin Goliath's pus,
eez stull tradin wile thare ah on thi broo
So git yir erse doon ti thi Seagate —
an see thi legend thitz JR
thirz no anybuddee even comes close —
but thirz jist naebiddee – on a level par
fae kail potz ti ornamental claes pegz,
in fact eez thare fir ah yir worldly needz
dinna spend yir sheckles in thi Hegh Street —
gie yir bizniss ti thi shop crehd…Jimmy Reid's!

BUSTERS
Anne MacDonald

A tuppeny buster
In a saucer
The Overgate smoky tent
Flap flung wide tae benches
An' faces weel kent
Peas an' ham in a cauldron
On a reekin' open flame
Stirred wi' heavy ladle
Far an' wide folk came

Chips fryin' in a pan
Dishes dichted in metal bath
On Saturdays, early fifties,
Footsteps trod the buster path

ON THE DISCOVERY OF A MASS GRAVE IN DUNDEE

Syd Scroggie

In 1651 me lads,
A blessed year of grace,
We Parliamentary soldiers came
And sat about this place.

And they were for the King me lads
And we were all for Noll,
And as for nests of Jacobites
That wouldn't do at all.

For they were sons of Baal they were
And blinkin' Ashtoreth,
And what was fit for such me lads,
Was something worse than death.

But we were soldiers of the Lord,
As pure as blinkin' lambs;
We fought with prayers and testaments
With sermons and with psalms.

We called the place Gomorrah lads
Where pagans held the Crown,
But those within another name;
They called it Dundee town.

They wouldn't change their ways me lads,
They wouldn't see the light,
So there was nothing else to do
But load our guns and fight.

We cannon'd down their walls me lads
We rushed their blinkin' gate,
We butchered Satan's myrmidons
And plundered gold and plate.

We chased them up the Overgait,
We chased them down the Well,
And when they cried for pity, sent
Them howling into Hell.

DUNDEE, 1651
Henry Marsh

Evening spans the firth to stain
the stubble rigs of Gowrie, fires
the clotted hips of the Burnet Rose.
In the thunder of His battering-pieces
God has spoken out of Sion. Where
the rag-polished sky of September
braided her pale wrists, violet
and purple orchid flower. Lips
in her throat gape. Flax bright,
her hair soaks in a poppy riot
on darkening cobbles. Who remarks
her infant's wailing? A wind drifts
God's flowers along the Overgait.
They spring from a fiery pillar, a steeple
uncrowned, as Governer Lumsden,
prisoner, some smouldering angel,
is felled by a pistol shot. Monck
looks on a Sabbath's work, ponders
a child's contribution to establishing
the reign of Christ upon the earth.

FROM THE GANGA TO THE TAY:
DUNDEE CONNECTION (EXCERPT)

Bashabi Fraser

So your indigenous
Corchorus
Was planted and
From March to May,
It grew to a glorious
Height of ten to twelve
Feet in its native domain.
Its yellow flowers
Succeeding summer heat,
Ready for the reaping
From July till October;
Its silky lustre
Gathered in bales
Of raw jute, heaping
Ships waiting
In your Bay
Which would later
Weave their way
From your port
Of Calcutta
To the city
of Dundee
On my banks,
Which, in its heyday
Was of first rank
And could boast
And give a toast
For being the hub
Of the gunny bag club –
Its thriving industry.

Ganga
But that was not
Till the 1830s
When my crops

Fed your factories
And Dundee led
The world trade
Processing fabrics
From my raw jute –
Dull brown sheets
Matted from the rubric
Of golden yarn
A success story
Spun out in
Cinderella splendour.
The near 40,000
Hundred weight
Of my billowing bales
Soared to dizzy heights
Of thirteen million
Which rose to more
In 1904,
Multiplying your sales
Beyond speculation
Or expectation
As goods from my lands
Reached your production arcades
And the rocketing tonnes
Linked our strands
By this golden skein.

Tay
Those massive bales
Of 400 pounds
Compressed by your
Hydraulic power
Were processed by
Cylinders and teeth
Into golden slivers
On my shores;
And later on yours,
Toned finer and finer

With fastidious combs
Then twisted into roves
Which, just like our
Distributaries, roam
Into diverse streams,
The warps with
The hard twist
Are swirled
In spools for
Dressing and starching
And reeled in hanks
Made ready for
Bleached futures
And coloured dreams
On factory looms –
Active on your shores.
And the wefts –
With the soft twist
Are put in neat cops
And thrust
Into bags for
Weaving
To follow in time.

THE FAMOUS TAY WHALE
William McGonagall

'TWAS in the month of December, and in the year 1883,
That a monster whale came to Dundee,
Resolved for a few days to sport and play,
And devour the small fishes in the silvery Tay.

So the monster whale did sport and play
Among the innocent little fishes in the beautiful Tay,
Until he was seen by some men one day,
And they resolved to catch him without delay.

When it came to be known a whale was seen in the Tay,
Some men began to talk and to say,
We must try and catch this monster of a whale,
So come on, brave boys, and never say fail.

Then the people together in crowds did run,
Resolved to capture the whale and to have some fun!
So small boats were launched on the silvery Tay,
While the monster of the deep did sport and play.

Oh! it was a most fearful and beautiful sight,
To see it lashing the water with its tail all its might,
And making the water ascend like a shower of hail,
With one lash of its ugly and mighty tail.

Then the water did descend on the men in the boats,
Which wet their trousers and also their coats;
But it only made them the more determined to catch the whale,
But the whale shook at them his tail.

Then the whale began to puff and to blow,
While the men and the boats after him did go,
Armed well with harpoons for the fray,
Which they fired at him without dismay.

And they laughed and grinned just like wild baboons,
While they fired at him their sharp harpoons:
But when struck with the harpoons he dived below,
Which filled his pursuers' hearts with woe.

Because they guessed they had lost a prize,
Which caused the tears to well up in their eyes;
And in that their anticipations were only right,
Because he sped on to Stonehaven with all his might:

And was first seen by the crew of a Gourdon fishing boat
Which they thought was a big coble upturned afloat;
But when they drew near they saw it was a whale,
So they resolved to tow it ashore without fail.

So they got a rope from each boat tied round his tail,
And landed their burden at Stonehaven without fail;
And when the people saw it their voices they did raise,
Declaring that the brave fishermen deserved great praise.

And my opinion is that God sent the whale in time of need,
No matter what other people may think or what is their creed;
I know fishermen in general are often very poor,
And God in His goodness sent it to drive poverty from their door.

So Mr John Wood has bought it for two hundred and twenty-six
pound,
And has brought it to Dundee all safe and all sound;
Which measures 40 feet in length from the snout to the tail,
So I advise the people far and near to see it without fail.

Then hurrah! for the mighty monster whale,
Which has got 17 feet 4 inches from tip to tip of a tail!
Which can be seen for a sixpence or a shilling,
That is to say, if the people all are willing.

DISCOVERY
Matthew Fitt

The RRS Discovery, yon widden thing wi roostit nails,
Rocks lichtlins noo in the Dundee herbour.

Worn awa beh hullfulls o Antartic ice scars,
Freezan sauty waaters an London sicht seers,
She laps, fuddilt an dune,
Hame in hur jaskit wastit wameskin.

An aa the aald widden ship discovert
In aa that time an aa thae places
Wis thit men that stey oot in the caald tae lang
Dee.

MID-CRAIGIE

A. D. Foote

The trees they planted here six years ago
Failed to take root.
Instead, the ground sprouted
Aerosols, dog turds, cans and bottles.
The middle-aged, who still remember the slums
Now older, pass by, hunch-backed,
Looking for something on the ground,

Something of value they lost long ago,
Before these fields were built upon.
Only the ever-living children shout and leap
At their unending play,

Growing up straight in a different world.

ON AN AULD HOOSE IN
THE COOGATE, DUNDEE

Athole Cameron

This is nae lyric land.
Nae heritage here
o kings an courtiers.
Echoes o trams
up the Victoria Road,
Reek o the mills,
Pinched faces abune claes
flecked wi poverty
an the raivellins o jute.
The sack-cloth city
in a snell wind
frae the Sidlaws tae the sea.

Nae landart loanin here,
Nae gait for grazin kye,
whaur Knox's wraith
at Wishart's Arch cries aye
the new dour faith,
that socht an pledged
nae quarter. Keen-edged,
his great twa-haunled sword,
as the bows o the whaling fleet.
The Broughty road rins yet
by Baffin Street.

GROWN UP
G.F. Dutton

three hundred tons of stone
each time, and its exploding
dust, and so has gone
Kirk Wynd and Caddengait,

unravelled to a lurch
and ashes, blown
high over shouting children
every afternoon.

Tam Gow's in that.
he drives a truck
and grins at them; looks great
in a yellow helmet.

SONG OF A DUNDEE LASS,
ON HER LOVER AT SEA
Robert Charles Dallas

Jemmy was a bonny lad,
    Well he pleugh'd his faither's glen,
But he cast away his plaid,
    To go fight with gallant men.
On the pleasant banks of Tay,
    Oft he told his love to me;
There he stole my heart away,
    The lad of bonny Dundee.

When he left the banks of Tay,
    Fame to seek among the brave,
Many a lass's heart was wae,
    But to me his troth he gave.
Maer to me his love than gold!
    And when Jemmy comes fra' sea,
To my bosom will I fold
    The lad of bonny Dundee.

APPLES
Kate Armstrong

A trace of salt in the air
and a south-facing slope
falling leaves everywhere
I take the back road in hope

of apples. Not to pick, but to find.
This stretch of land was set apart
For orchards, once. Now the road's lined
with brambles, birch and gean. The apples were the heart.

They were bred for early fruit, late flower
and just this soil. Their names are little known –
Tower of Glamis, Bloody Ploughman, Lass o Gowrie –
and they grow. They go on.

Few orchards remain, but in rough
land between tidy villages, so smart
with their two-car driveways, there's enough
space for the trees to lurk, the seeds to start

unseen. You need to look. You need to wait.
Stand around. Here it comes, a bit of a breeze
and bright apples roll on tarmac, gold, scarlet,
from the scraggy, almost-hidden trees.

And in the ancient sheds where ladders crumble
and wooden trays decay, pruning-hooks rust,
there are no skilled hands now. These sheds will tumble
soon, un-noticed, and turn to dust.

I crouch over the apples, cup my hand
on fairy-tale, and lift one to my mouth.
It smells of magic, tastes of nothing known. I stand
and turn my face to the south.

THE GREAT CAMPERDOWN BREAKOUT
W.N. Herbert

'A Dundee City Council spokesman described the wallabies
as not dangerous animals.'
(The Courier, 15.7.99)

Tho Camperdoon Park's a rare auld zoo,
nae baist, Eh think, gets pissed in there:
haal up a chair and Eh'll tell ye hoo
thir wallabies went oan thi tear.

Fehv broon, twa grey, and yin aa white,
these drongoes wi a drouth fur yill
louped owre thi fence at thi fit o thi night –
thir splores and spills ur aa meh tale.

They scellit, lyk The Great Escape,
tae spite thae parkies in pursuit:
wore shellsuits tae disguise thir shape
but luked a wee bit, well, hirsute.

No that ye'll no find men that hairy
if you sup beer in fair Lochee,
in Kirkton, tae, or in St Mary's,
fowk let thir follicles flow free.

But when fehv big broon wallaby bucks
hopped intae a bar in mirror specs,
there werr as mony muttirt 'fuck!'s
as oardirs fur pints o Fower X.

This wiz thi Sportin Lodge, whaur lads
ur not averse tae fisticuffs –
as bairns they'd battled in thir tansads,
but marsupials haund oot muckle duffs.

Wee manky Mike wiz furst tae swing,
and duntit thi snot fae a broonie's neb.
Ut geed a 'Tut,' syne sic a ding
Mike's een werr frehd lyk drappit eggs.

Thi boys piled in, thi wallabies
jist helt thir pints abune thir heids,
and wi thir tails they walloped these
sons o Lochee wi nae remeid.

They lunted owre the killiemahou,
got lowndered by lubbards, but paikit thi punks,
till mamikeekies, bluid and spew,
droukit this drave o roos and drunks.

Meanwhile a mannie, waur fur wear,
wiz stottin hame fae thi Golden Pheasant
when he saw a grey thing that lukeit mair
alien than usual in Harestane Crescent.

(Some sey these pubs ur nae langer there
and new wans hae sprung up i thi meantime,
while ithers feel thi haill affair
tuke place in an alcoholic Dreamtime.)

Ut spangit alang thi lane sae fast
ut seemed a ghaistly meteorite:
he stauchirt in thi hoose aghast
till his wife explained he wiz talkin shite.

Amanda awoke in Claverhoose Court
tae see a Greychops appear tae stare
thru'ur windie, then drap – wance mair fur sport,
no bad, since she bideit oan thi fourth flair.

A baker's drehvur in Edison Place
hud seen a grey, lyk young Amanda:
he'd backed tae thi circle and therr werr thi police –
sae he telt a Panda he'd spottit a kanga.

Thi parkies hud coarnered in Clatto Wuid
thae reprobates that bust up thi bar
when Doonfield Golf Course caaed that they hud
thir grey mate gaun roond at fehv under par.

Nae clubs as ye've guessed, he jist yaised his tail,
and blootert thi baas at thi boys in blue
till Tayside's finest turnit pale,
hid ahent shields and let him pley through.

Thi parkies flung nets aa nicht, and missed
till thi wallabies werr sae whammilt wi spreeins
(and mair by noo nor normal pished)
they gote caucht by these fishers of antipodeans.

Aa but thon brankless blank ane that
meh smarter hearers may still mind o
thi whitely wan, thon anti-bat,
oor flit-by-nicht Dick Whitterton – kind o –

Ned Kelter o thi Seedlie Hills,
thi wallaby that won awa,
that wool Houdini-whale whas skills
huv made wee Ahabs of us aa.

Snow Joey, hoo yir freends noo languish
and gee wir visitors thi Skippy finger:
they say 'Come hame,' in sober language –
thir heids ur nippin fae thon humdinger.

Thon reilibogie really blew
their brains and oors oot Alice Springs-way:
thir pooches ur fuhl o Irn Bru,
thir mooths o tarmac fae thi Kingsway.

But still Eh see him in a dwaum
gae hoppin owre thi purple braes,
thon aboriginal wee bam:
Eh hope he stubs his fuckin taes.

4
THE TYPES

BONNY DUNDEE

Sir Walter Scott

To the Lords of Convention 'twas Claver'se who spoke.
'Ere the King's crown shall fall there are crowns to be broke;
So let each Cavalier who loves honour and me,
Come follow the bonnet of Bonny Dundee.
Come fill up my cup, come fill up my can,
Come saddle your horses, and call up your men;
Come open the West Port and let me gang free,
And it's room for the bonnets of Bonny Dundee!'

Dundee he is mounted, he rides up the street,
The bells are rung backward, the drums they are beat;
But the Provost, douce man, said, 'Just e'en let him be,
The Gude Toun is weel quit of that Deil of Dundee.'

As he rode down the sanctified bends of the Bow,
Ilk carline was flyting and shaking her pow;
But the young plants of grace they looked couthie and slee,
Thinking luck to thy bonnet, thou Bonny Dundee!

With sour-featured Whigs the Grass-market was crammed,
As if half the West had set tryst to be hanged;
There was spite in each look, there was fear in each e'e,
As they watched for the bonnets of Bonny Dundee.

These cowls of Kilmarnock had spits and had spears,
And lang-hafted gullies to kill cavaliers;
But they shrunk to close-heads and the causeway was free,
At the toss of the bonnet of Bonny Dundee.

He spurred to the foot of the proud Castle rock,
And with the gay Gordon he gallantly spoke;
'Let Mons Meg and her marrows speak twa words or three,
For the love of the bonnet of Bonny Dundee.'

The Gordon demands of him which way he goes —
'Where'er shall direct me the shade of Montrose!
Your Grace in short space shall hear tidings of me,
Or that low lies the bonnet of Bonny Dundee.

'There are hills beyond Pentland and lands beyond Forth,
If there's lords in the Lowlands, there's chiefs in the North;
There are wild Duniewassals three thousand times three,
Will cry hoigh! for the bonnet of Bonny Dundee.

'There's brass on the target of barkened bull-hide;
There's steel in the scabbard that dangles beside;
The brass shall be burnished, the steel shall flash free,
At the toss of the bonnet of Bonny Dundee.

'Away to the hills, to the caves, to the rocks —
Ere I own an usurper, I'll couch with the fox;
And tremble, false Whigs, in the midst of your glee,
You have not seen the last of my bonnet and me!'

He waved his proud hand, the trumpets were blown,
The kettle-drums clashed and the horsemen rode on,
Till on Ravelston's cliffs and on Clermiston's lee
Died away the wild war-notes of Bonny Dundee.
Come fill up my cup, come fill up my can,
Come saddle the horses, and call up the men,
Come open your gates, and let me gae free,
For it's up with the bonnets of Bonny Dundee!

GRIZZEL JAFFRAY

Joseph Lee

The burning of the last of the Dundee witches at the Mercat Cross in the Seagate, November 1669.

'Come out, come out, Grizzel Jaffray,
　For thy black gramarye;
Come out, come out, Grizzel Jaffray,
　To-day but thou maun dee.

'Come out, come out, foul witch Jaffray;
　Or e'er the nicht return,
Thy body wirried at the stake
　In flames o' hell shall burn.'

She's taen her aik staff in her hand,
　And out-stapped to the door;
And but and she is bowed and bent
　Wi' years anigh fourscore.

'Come out, come out, Grizzel Jaffray,
　Come out, come out,' they cry;
'Thy soul is barter'd to the de'il,
　Thou hast the evil eye.'

'O, I am bent and bow'd,' quo' she,
　'And dim my fading een,
Wi' length o' years that I hae lived,
　Wi' sorrow I hae seen.'

'Out on thee, witch Grizzel Jaffray,
　Out on thy evil eye;
Whilk gar't Roy's bairnie waste awa,
　And Kirstie's coo gang dry.'

And one was there who smote her cheek,
  Nor did she blast nor ban;
But said, 'E'en so the soldiers smote
  The blessed Son of Man.'

They have taen her to the Witches' Pool,
  To see if she would droon;
And the waters went not ower her head,
  But the current bare her roun'.

'If my stout son had been at hame,
  As he is on the sea,
The bauldest men amang ye a'
  Had not put this shame on me.'

They have taen her to the Mercat Cross,
  To see if she would burn;
And ere the flames came ower her head
  A ship she did discern.

'If that were but my son's stout ship,
  As it is on the sea,
There's nane the bravest o' them a',
  Dare have put this death on me.'

The ship has steered into port,
  And the Captain come on shore;
'Now tell me true, my bonnie boy,
  What means this loud uproar?

'And what was that strange licht I saw,
  As I steeréd for Dundee,
Which rose and fell, beside the Cross,
  As it would beckon me?'

'Then up and spake that bonnie boy,
  In tones of meikle glee,
'O, Witch Grizzel Jaffray is burned —
And I hae seen her dee!

'What aileth thee, strange Marinere?
  I fear thy look so wild!'
'Nay, little it becometh me
  T' affright a simple child.

'O, mither, had I been at hame,
  As I was on the sea,
There's nane the bravest o' them a'
  Had laid this death on thee.

'How often from the cauld and heat,
  Has thou been shield to me,
And yet from these same cruel fires
  I might not succour thee!

'O, God, that their black souls may burn,
  Deep, deep, in reddest hell,
Wha burnt they body at the stake —
  Sweet mother, fare-thee-well!'

He's put his good ship round about,
  And out steered for the sea;
And lang the years have come and gane,
  But nae mair hame cam' he.

Tradition has it that a son of Grizzel Jaffray, a master mariner, put in to Dundee with his ship on the very day of his mother's burning, and learning what had happened, at once set sail and was never heard of again.

DAFT DAVIE

(A TRUE TALE)
William Beharrie

Ance on a time daft Davie Begg
When he was in the as'lum,
Sairly did his keeper fleg
The followin is the outcum.

A poor demented inmate there
Slipet had life's cable,
An' a' that after death remains
Was streekit on a table.

The keeper left for Coffin Tam
The measure o' him to tak,
Just left the door aff the sneck
Thocht he wud soon be back.

Davie daundrin throu' the place
Espied the door a jee,
An' kennin o' the corp being there
Thocht he'd gang in and see.

He looket roun an' roun the dead
An' scanned the body o'er,
Keeket cautious round the place
An' syne drew to the door,

An' straught began to strip the corp
O' a' its hinmost claes,
Till stark an' stiff without a rag
To cover tap or taes.

Then a' his ain he shuffl'd aff
Left naething, no a stockin,
And dress'd the corp in his ain suit
O wisna that most shockin!

But Davie thought a fair exchange
Could ne'er be countit stealin.
He clappit on the deadman's claes
Without a thought or feelin.

He set the corp upon a chair
Up in the farest nook,
And turn'd its face forenent the wa'
And placed in its hand a book.

Then on the table laid himsell
Where lay the dead before,
Compos'd himsell as he were dead
But anxious watch'd the door.

Nor very lang had he to wait
Sune he heard them cumin,
To play his part to flegg the twa
Did a' his courage summin.

When in they came and look't roun
They thought 'twas Davie readin,
And speer'd at him what brought him here
But Davie ne'er was heedin.

Ye born idiot, the keeper cried
Hae ye been after stealin?
Then taen him in th'lug a crack
That sent the corp a reelin.

Then up bang'd the corp as they thought
Wow what a gruesome carl!
And spake in hollow tones an' said
This is an Awfu Warl!

They never staid to tak ae look
But fled the place for fear,
They coupit ither in the haste
An' tumbild doun the stair.

They left daft Davie wi' the dead
Ance mair to shift the claes,
I'm thinkin lads ye got a flegg
Ye'll mind on a' yer days.

DEATH OF A COMIC ARTIST
C.B. Donald

They find his final strip still incomplete
with deadlines on the table for this week;
pen still gripped in white-knuckled grasp,
slumped while drawing in a comic gasp.

A junior staffer imitates his hand
so only fans can spot the difference,
and they're too young to understand
the effort they buy for their sixpence.

Readers giggle at those last hi-jinks:
the desperate closing moments of his Dan.
They never quite discern that his last words
are filled in by another, lesser, man.

It doesn't bother eager readers,
torches beneath midnight sheets,
that the ink is still wet on his obituary.

PAINTING BY NUMBERS

for J Campbell Kerr

Andy Jackson

In the loft of the red Lubyanka, at the crown
of the Kingsway, there's a studio, cool and bright,
where the painter sits, stealing the ochre-brown
from blisters of rock in the outback, spiriting white
from the blankness of polar ice and snowmelt rush,
liberating sweltered greens and yellows from the veldt,
forging the blue of fluke and fin, rust of Sahara dusk,
the counterfeited black from notches in Orion's belt.

His loaded brushwork saturates the knock-off scenes
that hail from platform kiosks or from trolleys
wheeled through long-stay wards; the magazines
that call themselves *your friend*. The haggard glory
of the harbourfront at Rothesay or the Moray Firth
are paraphrased in Polynesian hues, poster-bold,
and yet in fugitive colours; a rendering of Earth
no single room or page or name could ever hold.

DAVIT DICK, DUNDEE CARRIER
John Smith

The truth lives lang wove in a sang,
    Nae hole in mine you'll pick;
Come on and try, ye critic fry,
    It's pointed 'up tae Dick.'

Ye Templar crew wi' ribbons blue
    Fecht weel an' war Auld Nick;
But oh, forbear, or fire in air.
    An' fricht not Davit Dick.

The honest man heeds not your ban;
    The spootreech you may kick,
Drone on like bees, or howl oot lees,
    But dave not Davit Dick.

Throughoot Dundee weel kent is he;
    There may be men mair slick,
But nane mair sure this day or 'oor
    Than steady Davit Dick.

O' toil an' care he's had his share;
    Still sticks in like a brick,
O'er road an' line sin' I can min',
    Aye at it Davit Dick.

Some plunge and splash, some cut a dash,
    Some ruin the warl' wi' tick;
Credit nor cash need merchants fash
    Were a' the folk like Dick.

But you shou'd see his sparklin' e'e
    Warmed wi' the rick-ma-tick;
Frae harness free a' heart is he,
    The auld laird, Davit Dick.

Gae 'wa' wi' wealth that's got by stealth,
    Or rogues that cut their stick;
He'll never boo tae ribbon blue
    Wha has a heart like Dick.

Time, grant him joy that will not cloy,
    His dud and his bit pick,
An' a wee drap tae moist his crap,
    The auld cock Davit Dick.

Tae perfect life he needs a wife;
    Though ladies hunt him thick,
He jokes awa' an' coorts them a'
    But wha'll be mistress Dick?

A canty hame for some trig dame;
    A blister yet micht stick.
Wha daur gainsay? He'll ne'er say nay
    The sprush beau Davit Dick.

We'll tak' a drap until we flap,
    Syne settle wi' Auld Nick;
Bring in a gill, a bumper fill,
    Here's tae ye! Davit Dick.

ETCHING OF A LINE OF TREES

i.m. John Goodfellow Glenday

John Glenday

I carved out the careful absence of a hill and a hill grew.
I cut away the fabric of the trees
and the trees stood shivering in the darkness.

When I had burned off the last syllables of wind,
a fresh wind rose and lingered.
But because I could not bring myself

to remove you from that hill,
you are no longer there. How wonderful it is
that neither of us managed to survive

when it was love that surely pulled the burr
and love that gnawed its own shape from the burnished air
and love that shaped that absent wind against a tree?

Some shadow's hands moved with my hands
and everything I touched was turned to darkness
and everything I could not touch was light.

CALL
G.F. Dutton

A furious wind
on the outer estates,
hail and sleet
at the high flats,

the street lights
flickering.
A good night
for visiting,

rummaging, trying
another's mind,
with something else
beating around

to think about,
to get in the talk.
Up at the door
two blocks back

held half-opened,
Jim and his wife,
his smile uneasy
hers the cool knife

sweet to remember.
Aye man come in,
Liz was just saying
you'd look along,

Christ what a bloody
hell of a wind.
He goes before me.
She behind.

THE HOOKERS OF DUNDEE

Harry Smart

In Dundee, where even the nightclubs
Have a certain ecclesiasticality of appearance,
The hookers are not particularly sophisticated.

The permafrost is not far away,
Therefore the hookers of Dundee
Cannot display much of their merchandise;

Not as much as the dummy at McGills'
Who displays a real snip, the Carlotti Badminton Set,
And who looks far more appealing than the hookers.

The hookers of Dundee favour such approaches
As almost falling over in front of the punters
Then giggling in a coarse fashion.

Like most things in Dundee,
Churches, nightclubs, nights on the town,
The hookers of Dundee are not particularly successful.

DUNDEE HAIKU
Kate Armstrong

Shoals of assistants
Jink in the fishpond behind
McLeish's counter

BREAKDOWN
Carl MacDougall

Mary broke down
outside Draffens.

She cried and cried
then sat on the pavement.

People stared
as they passed.

Some looked
as though she was drunk.

Someone asked
if she was all right

or if she fancied
a wee drink

and someone else
threw money.

THE CHEAPO HAIRDRESSER
UP HORSEWATER WYND
David Strachan

Ah went tae the cheapo hairdresser up Horsewater Wynd theday.

Fir lang enough A've been cutting ma ain hair
wi Agnes antlin on an on aboot it,
till this morning,
maistly jist tae snite her nib,
Ah hurkled doon tae the cheapo hairdresser
up Horsewater Wynd.

A cauf-lick'd man wis sweepin up the mornin's crop o hair.
A gash-gabbit wumman wis sittin
wi her haunds half-shut, glowerin at her nails.
A radio on the sink wis playin Jimmy Shand.

Ah got the gash-mou'd wumman.

Whit's a this? she speared,
tugtuggin the tufts at the back o ma heid.
Wha's been here afore me, lad?
Ah mumbled that Ah'd done it masel.
O, she said, cruikin her mou,
yir wan o thaim. Hear that, Bert?
He's wan o thaim!
an she flapped a white cape thing roon me,
wrappin me up ticht.
Weel weel. An hoo diz Maister Beckham want it?
Tapered, crestit, crinkled, or whit?
Ah asked her jist tae tidy it up a bit.
O ah'll tidy it up, she said,
Trust me. Ah'll tidy it up fur ye aw richt.

The man pit his besom doon tae watch,
the wumman circling, snippin, tousling,
croonin awa tae herself in time tae the Jimmy Shand,
touslin awa wi ae haund,

clipclipclippin wi the ither,
hair cascading roon her like sna in a bleester.

Ah kept ma een doon,
watchin the backs o ma haunds turn intae a werewolf's.

Weel then, she said at last, aw hinnie an an jo noo,
haudin a mirror up ahint ma heid
so Ah could admire the fou extent o her artistry.
whit dae ye think?

Ah said nothing, paid her, geid her a tip,
an managed no tae howl till Ah got hame.

PEGGY
Dorothy Lawrenson

In the first days of the year
they made a fleeting visit.

They'd not stop long.

Alec stood at the gate
while Peg stayed in the car;
that's my memory of her,
stuck in the passenger seat,
baggy, immobile by then.
I was maybe eight, and a logical
connection formed with mum's
bulky old peg-bag, shirt-shaped
to hang on the line, an everyday,
awe-inspiring sight.

Decades since she'd worked a loom
 – in Dundee, a *limb*
like an extension of the body;
one woman might work three or four,
dancing shifting bobbins
among the din and the dust.

Back then she was adamant:
'They say weavers shout
but we dinnae shout;
we can aw lipread!'
 – then she'd break off and bawl
from her fourth floor window
to the bairns in the court below.

And the wailing o the bummer and the clacking o the looms
brought the women o Dundee oot o their beds;

their singing sounds
across a century,
their coarse beauty
strong as spun jute.

That's my memory of Peg:
frozen in space and time
as if ready for the off –
a sack-full of the past, to be glimpsed
then whisked away.

They'd not stop long.

DELUSIONS OF GRANDEUR
A. D. Foote

'Oh yes, I've been to Spitsbergen', he said,
'Built myself a hut from the ship's timbers
With my bare hands:
We lived on meat from a whale's carcass
Stranded on the shore.'

Next day I happened to mention Tenerife.
He'd been there as well.
'The native girls wear roses behind their ears
That they give to any stranger
They want to spend the night with.'

When he had been a month on the ward
It came out
He had never ever been in Dundee
Except for a night he spent in the police-cell
On the way to hospital.

Then when he did go
He lost his way between City Square and the bus-stop
And had to be brought back
In an ambulance.

'It's not at all like Siberia,' he ruefully confided,
'There you can follow the trails the reindeer make
For miles across the tundra
Until you reach your base.'

It would be satisfying to relate
That he ended by pushing off
To China or the Antarctic,
But in fact he, strangely, got better
And now works in a jute-mill
Off the Perth Road.

THE LONESOME DEATH
OF FRANCIS CLARKE

Michael Marra

There is a place out in the Yukon
Lying there, a shipwright's bones
By his side his adze and compass
And by his feet there is a curling stone
Lying by his feet there is a curling stone.

A fountain pen lies in his waistcoat
Although they found no written farewell
He died on a night that was cold as his family
Oh it was icy at the Gates of Hell
Surprised that it was icy at the Gates of Hell.

Fare thee well, brave Uncle Francis
When the snowflakes fall I will sing the blues
And when I think of how you left this world
I will remember how the world left you.

They say he fell for an Indian maiden
Who was more lovely that mere words could tell
He lay in her arms and they bathed in the moonlight
He softly sang of the Bailieborough Belle
He sang to the maiden of the Bailieborough Belle.

Fare thee well, brave Uncle Francis
When the snowflakes fall I will sing the blues
And when I think of how you left this world
I will remember how the world left you.

And who among us would still say
I'll not forgive until my dying day
Between the Earth and Sky above
There must be a twinkling seam of love.

I'll summon up the drums of the Blackness Foundry
Blind Mattie, the Mackay twins too
We'll sing it up from the Overgate to Anchorage
And place a coal upon the fire for you
We'll place a precious coal upon the fire for you.

Fare thee well, brave Uncle Francis
When the snowflakes fall I will sing the blues
And when I think of how you left this world
I will remember how the world left you.

And when I think of how you left this world
I will remember how the world left you.

KING O' THE LAW
The Roper Bard

Oh! bonnie Law Hill! oh, bonnie Law Hill,
When I was a loonie lang syne at the mill,
I've climbed to thy tap in my innocent glee,
Alang wi' my wee mates, my draigen to flee;
My draigen was biggest and never broke line,
For I had the langest an' strongest o' twine;
It was my ambition to oot-flee them a'
That mine might be titled the King o' the Law.

Oh, bonnie Law Hill! oh, bonnie Law Hill!
E'en noo frae thy tap I can see the auld mill!
Whaurin I wrought weel till I entered my teens
Amang my work mates at the hackle machines.
On summer's clear nichts when oor day's wark was dune,
We gaed to the Law, doffed oor stockins an' shune;
At rinnin' an' jumpin' I whiles beat them a' –
'Twas grand to be titled the King o' the Law.

Oh, bonnie Law Hill! oh, bonnie Law Hill!
I'd like fine to ken if my mates are a' still
In the land o' the livin'; if ony there be,
I winner if ever they mind aboot me.
It's thirty lang years sin oor draigens we flew –
Hoo short the time seems when the past we review –
They surely a' canna be dead an' awa'
Wha played there an' ca'd me the King o' the Law.

Oh, bonnie Law Hill! oh, bonnie Law Hill!
Time soon will the prophet's three sayin's fulfil;
Auld Tammas, the Rhymer, declared ye wad be
Some time in the future the heart o' Dundee.
Ships sail on the sea noo without the wind force,
An' cars on the streets noo are drawn withoot horse;
I winner if ony when I'm tane awa'
Will ever remember the King o' the Law.

CHILDREN SLEDDING IN THE DARK, MAGDALEN GREEN
John Burnside

We have studied the colours of night:
loan-path ambers, hedges dipped in bronze,
jade-tinted snow

and nothing is wholly true
till we believe:
the sky is glass, the distance is a train,

angels are sealed in the gaps
of walls, their fledged wings
spreading through mortar,

and under the lamps, possessed by the pull of the dark,
these children hold the glow
of the imagined,

perfect and hard, arriving at copper or gold
by guesswork; trusting what's contrived in flesh
to echo in the rooms of gravity.

TAY BRIDGE, NIGHT
Valerie Gillies

Our train and passengers spin at a height
above sea level, it bottles us
up at the launch of the night.
We grow momentous.
Across ravelling space
piers and girders link,
eyes shine outside, a face
on the blink.

Skeletons make no fuss
when they join arms with us.
If we look vain
they lead us in the train
of their steelbone embrace.
Combining at this point in space,
Strange couplings, these:
Youth and joy, fear and disease.
We who are full
of life will fall.
The bony ones arrest
us, clasped to their gridiron chests,
as to the unexpected mate
we feel the pull and gravitate.

REANEY
Andrew Murray Scott

And when Reaney talked
The redsea waters of our ears
Divided and were strange
In a backroom bar in the Hawkhill.

The Old Tav; it was late '73,
Sawdust, rickety chairs, beerspills
on polished wooden counters,
Streetlight smoking redly through the optics.

Duffle-coated days of denim,
Autumn evening air wafting
Like memory the fuggy smoke
Finding us lit in the back snug.

Further in cantos of hoarse whispers
In stanzaic tread, with bardic joy
He assigned us an antique eloquence;
Our Dylan Thomas (of Hilltown Terrace).

Pints were his punctuation
Players No 6 his mystic wand
Losing us in the pages of Ulysses,
Or among the islands of Tir Nan Og.

But when Willie's bell rang last orders,
It now seemed a death knell
Of all the bright possibilities
In our world, of friends we knew

Long since curtailed, too soon –
Too many and all but forgotten.

And Reaney? Ah, Reaney…

NATIONAL POETRY DAY
Lydia Robb

It's National Poetry Day today
says the faceless man over the tannoy.
There will be readings on the first
and second floors of the Centre.

Christ! There's me on CCTV.
Drop the dead dactyl.

For my next appearance ... I will
foot it up the down escalator,
jingle the turnstile at the ladies loo,
rap around the Wellgate clock,
lampoon the punters in their tracks.

It's not like that at all. I'm trying
my damnedest to remain invisible.

Measure the reaction.
Two deaf pensioners,
a few open-mouthed schoolkids
and me scanning the shoppers
for one interested face.
Heroic or what?

The glass doors tick, tick then cut.
I'm out, into the concrete poem
of the Hilltown.

LEAVING DUNDEE
Douglas Dunn

A small blue window opens in the sky
As thunder rumbles somewhere over Fife.
Eight months of up-and-down – goodbye, goodbye –
Since I sat listening to the wild geese cry
Fanatic flightpaths up autumnal Tay,
Instinctive, mad for home – make way! make way!
Communal feathered scissors, cutting through
The grievous artifice that was my life,
I was alert again, and listening to
That wavering, invisible V-dart
Between two bridges. Now, in a moistened puff,
Flags hang on the chateau-stacked gables of
A 1980s expense account hotel,
A lost French fantasy, baronial,
From here, through the trees, its Frenchness hurts my heart.
It slips into a library of times.
Like an eye on a watch, it looks at me.
And I am going home on Saturday
To my house, to sit at my desk of rhymes
Among familiar things of love, that love me.
Down there, over the green and the railway yards,
Across the broad, rain-misted subtle Tay,
The road home trickles to a house, a door.
She spoke of what I might to 'afterwards'.
'Go, somewhere else.' I went north to Dundee.
Tomorrow I won't live here any more,
Nor leave alone. *My love, say you'll come with me.*

THESE THINGS
Dylan Drummond

in the laundrette on the Lochee Road
these things
you in a bright green dress shimmering like those rigorous few
    blades of grass
that somehow manage to elude the looming shadows of creeping
    dusk on the lawn
the old man perpetually angry at having to adjust his head as he
    conceals the fact
that he slides his vision over your form but only when your patient
    eyes are perfectly hidden
four particularly obese flies dancing in the heat high up out of reach
noisier than teeth each frantic to fill the void
that is left behind the swooning and resurrection of the three others
a couple of scruffy kids and yet another with broken leg extended
    in wheelchair
claiming sanctuary as they distribute the pirate bounty of their
    days shoplifting
the restlessness of sharing silence with strangers
the billowing of clouds of steam out on to the pavement
and steady mantra of the passing traffic pounding against the huge
    plate glass
that contains us
all that which passes us seems to be going nowhere or everywhere
all these things unconnected
telling no discernible story
casual events astray in a tumbling universe
you lifting effortlessly your warm arms
filling your space the way you tend to do.

ON THE DUNDEE BUS
Honor Patching

We hang in this bus like herrings in the smoke,
Elbow to elbow, as though the whole of Fife
Were traveling, pickled in ammoniac reek
Of babies' nappies. Twisting, I rub a sleeve
Against the window where I'm crammed. Misted
Glass smears, I glimpse a blur of trees,
Craning my neck beneath *No Smoking* pasted
At eye-height. Across the Tay, Dundee's
Blue-wet runs, smudges smoke and sky.
Rust-red, an oil-rig wades against the water's
Metal. A wide light runs frosty
Clear to the river. Like mothers and daughters
In damp headscarves, lapwings land, all
A-flutter, to probe for worms, their scraps of scandal.

THE WORTHIES O' DUNDEE
F. W. Swan

There was a man called Waterloo
    That carried a muckle stick,
And if you cried out Paddy's craw
    You was sure to get a lick.

Peter Powrie and Jelly Feet,
    And Sneeky Moo and his brot,
And Trokie Knows, and Docherty,
    And his face as clean's the pot.

There was Humphy Kate and fechtin' Nell,
    And drucken Andrew Buddie,
Brimstane Bet and skipper Bell,
    And Saut and Whitening's cuddie.

Tattie Jean and Fiddler Tam,
    And sporting Fanny Brown,
Policeman Scobbie and Gashie Taws
    Then the hale force o' this town.

Daft Nosey Jack and Hairy Kale,
    The bellman o' the Hill,
Blind Andrew Drummond, that often sang
    The Lass o' Patie's Mill.

Daft Magdalene and Fire Nannie,
    And Daft Jean Tyrie too,
And Humphie Jonnie wi' his blue,
    And the Showman Mealy Poo.

Dazy Ingram and Dozzy Lamb,
    And Rusty Needles and Preens,
Fluckes and Treacle the dirty man,
    Mrs Stalker and her greens,

And ane amang the conncil
    Was little Willie Blair,
The laird o' Tipperary,
    For an MP he tried sair.

Blind Hughie too, we canna pass,
    For he had sangs in store;
Ye can mind the bellman wi' the ass
    And Razor at the shore.

Fizzie Gow the showman,
    Betty Blair that selled the tripe,
Birdie Hynd the cobbler,
    Mrs Lyall the big fish wife.

Auld John Dye the chimney sweep,
    Stormont the auctioneer,
Mick Leaburn in the market,
    And Baker the big lear.

Joe Dempster the bellman,
    Cried the empty bag wi' the cheese,
Johnny Wood, the merchant
    That deals amang the greese.

Fat Keiller and Saut Cowan,
    Twa cautious market chaps,
Charlie Harris the bellman,
    Mrs Grant among her slops.

Take-an-egg Mearns.
    And little Piloty Tosh,
Tarry Jack and Cowheel,
    The cooper Tammy Ross.

John Neucater and his scutcher,
    And captain Johnny Lee,
The oldest skipper in the trade
    Between Kingoodie and Dundee.

Tam Wighton and Cripple Crichton,
      Dilce Charlie and his barrow,
Candy Kate and Taffy Reid,
      The carter Willie Harrie.

London Spices, Geordie Sweeney,
      The Russian Geordie Crow,
And Sweetie Tammy Tenant,
      That lived in Thorter Row.

Little Jocky Alexander
      And Brand that sold the saut,
Tripe Shearer into Fish Street,
      And a pub called John o' Groat.

Parochial Johnny Coogan,
      And Beadle some called Ross,
If you do not pay your rates
      They showed you they were boss.

Mr Leng the king o' papers,
      And praying Davie Begg,
Scabbie Joe and Langshanks
      The ghost o' Chapelshade.

Captain Davie Edwards
      O' the Star o' Tay,
Jock Elphiston the scraper,
      And little Jockey May.

Big John Bog the beagle,
      To roup you he wasna shy,
Charlie Walker the cadger,
      The jailer Couter Mackay.

James M Fu the lawyer,
      And sporting Flowerdew,
Lang Tam Abbot the beagle,
      And detective Jamie Dow.

Hill, the lovely tenant,
    Mackie upon his horse,
Mr Parr and Mr Lamb,
    Our consequential force.

King Coffee and Heather Heels,
    Among the common tribe.
Beveridge and Naigge
    Their high horse full doth ride.

Brownlee, ex-Provost,
    That put himself into a state,
Gave Peter Graham the hundred pounds
    For stealing the silver plate.

Mr Bisset the beagle,
    No a bad-hearted loon,
And canny Mungo Ritchie,
    Big Steel that kept the Crown.

Jockey Stewart the runner,
    Sandy Fields the crimp,
Bobbie Waddle the tailor,
    A cheeky little imp.

Poor Mag Gow the cadger,
    And the Female Jack Mackay,
McGonegal the poet,
    Kitty Luckie wi' her kye.

Funny Tammy Fraser,
    Little fat cabby Gray,
Drunken Willie Christopher,
    The showman Mr Day.

P. O'Niel professor,
    Robbie Salmond wi' his bread,
Sold sweeties, gingerbread, a' in lots,
    At sixpence overhead.

Black Mag and Tammy Tamson,
　　Pie Snaps into the Hill,
And Muckle Nosey Anderson,
　　That wrought in Dease's Mill.

Mr Arthur the scavenger,
　　And sanitary Tam Kinnear,
That made his wife so odious,
　　To divorce her he tried sair.

Honey Tam the cadger
　　Slout Cooper and Stout Scott,
Cripple Willie and Piper Cameron,
　　Tumley Down the drunken sot

Collins the comedian,
　　And Mr D. B. Brown,
And Rennie the policeman,
　　That kept the cheepers down.

Mr George O'Farrell,
　　A man that kept a pop,
And Muckle Bubbly Tammy,
　　And Livingston the fop.

The great Gilroy, a spinner,
　　The provost wi' his ale,
He was a man of consequence,
　　And no like Neelie Steel.

The ane sold ale in pitchers,
　　The other an ounce of tea,
Neelie sold to auld wives,
　　The ither to the ragtag o' Dundee.

And sturdy Bailie Gentle,
　　A man wi' lots o' sense,
He liked aye to ha'e a shine,
　　But at the town's expense.

Jock Rattray and his auld horse,
 And carter Muzzel Joe,
And Simpson wi' his bagpipes,
 He prided them to blow.

And cheeky Mr Piper Gray,
 But we mauna him despise,
Daft Baubie, Nae Luck that way,
 And Athole wi' his pies.

Jock Maxwell and his apples,
 Fish cadger Andrew Dand,
Bobbie Clement, and Tailor Third,
 A cheeky little man

…

But of a' the lot I mentioned here,
 Of worthies great and sma',
Pie Jock's been up and in the moon,
 To see a' what was there,

But of a' the lot I mentioned here,
 Of worthies great and sma',
Pie Jock's been up and in the moon,
 Wi' Jock o' Aranha'

Twa Jocks they had a gill or twa
 Frae a man into the air
Then they entered in the moon
 To see a' what was there,

There was lots o' thieves and hangmen,
 Reading the *Weekly News*,
And lots o' lein' policemen,
 Mrs Collins and Skipper Blues.

There were ministers and lawyers,
    And doctors there also,
And lots o' them that couldna live
    At peace wi' us below.

The same twa worthies had a booze,
    Pie Jock he wanted hame,
And through the clouds cam' tumblin' down,
    And landed in Trades Lane.

THE LASS O' GOWRIE
Carolina, Lady Nairne

'Twas on a simmer's afternoon,
A wee afore the sun gaed doun,
A lassie wi' a braw new goun
    Cam' owre the hills to Gowrie.
The rosebud washed in simmer's shower
Bloomed fresh within the sunny bower;
But Kitty was the fairest flower
    That e'er was seen in Gowrie.

To see her cousin she cam' there;
An' oh! the scene was passing fair,
For what in Scotland can compare
    Wi' the Carse o' Gowrie?
The sun was setting on the Tay,
The blue hills melting into gray,
The mavis and the blackbird's lay
    Were sweetly heard in Gowrie.

O lang the lassie I had wooed,
And truth and constancy had vowed,
But could na' speed wi' her I lo'ed
    Until she saw fair Gowrie.
I pointed to my faither's ha' –
Yon bonnie bield ayont the shaw,
Sae loun' that there nae blast could blaw: –
    Wad she no bide in Gowrie?

Her faither was baith glad and wae;
Her mither she wad naething say;
The bairnies thocht they wad get play
    If Kitty gaed to Gowrie.
She whiles did smile, she whiles did greet;
The blush and tear were on her cheek;
She naething said, an' hung her head; –
    But now she's Leddy Gowrie.

BURIAL OF THE REV. GEORGE GILFILLAN

William McGonagall

On the Gilfillan burial day,
In the Hill o' Balgay,
It was a most solemn sight to see,
Not fewer than thirty thousand people assembled in Dundee,
All watching the funeral procession of Gilfillan that day,
That death had suddenly taken away,
And was going to be buried in the Hill o' Balgay.

There were about three thousand people in the procession alone,
And many were shedding tears, and several did moan,
And their bosoms heaved with pain,
Because they knew they would never look upon his like again.

There could not be fewer than fifty carriages in the procession that
      day,
And gentlemen in some of them that had come from far away,
And in whispers some of them did say,
As the hearse bore the precious corpse away,
Along the Nethergate that day.
I'm sure he will be greatly missed by the poor,
For he never turned them empty-handed away from his door;
And to assist them in distress it didn't give him pain,
And I'm sure the poor will never look upon his like again.

On the Gilfillan burial day, in the Hill o' Balgay,
There was a body of policemen marshalled in grand array
And marched in front of the procession all the way;
Also the relatives and friends of the deceas'd,
Whom I hope from all sorrows has been releas'd,
and whose soul I hope to heaven has fled away,
To sing with saints above for ever and aye.

The provost, magistrates, and town council were in the procession
      that day;
Also Mrs Gilfillan, who cried and sobbed all the way
For her kind husband, that was always affable and gay,

Which she will remember until her dying day.

When the procession arrived in the Hill o' Balgay,
The people were almost as hush as death, and many of them did
    say —
As long as we live we'll remember the day
That the great Gilfillan was buried in the Hill o' Balgay.

When the body of the great Gilfillan was lowered into the grave,
'Twas then the people's hearts with sorrow did heave;
And with tearful eyes and bated breath,
Mrs Gilfillan lamented her loving husband's death.

Then she dropped a ringlet of immortelles into his grave,
Then took one last fond look, and in sorrow did leave;
And all the people left with sad hearts that day,
And that ended the Gilfillan burial in the Hill o' Balgay.

DUNDEE'S OWN

Anonymous (The People's Journal, 11 December 1915)

The day you marched away,
  Dundee's Own,
Our hearts were like to break,
  Dundee's Own,
But you smiled away our tears,
And stifled all our fears,
Changing them to ringing cheers
  For Dundee's Own.

When Neuve Chapelle was o'er,
  Dundee's Own,
We gloried in your deeds,
  Dundee's Own!
For we knew the town's good name
Had been honoured by your fame,
You had bravely played the game
  For Dundee's Own!

But alas our hearts are sad,
  Dundee's Own.
We mourn your sleeping brave,
  Dundee's Own.
Mid the storm of shot and shell
Where gallant heroes fell
There lie broken hearts as well
  With Dundee's Own.

When victorious you march home,
  Dundee's Own,
To the city proud to call you
  Dundee's Own,
If we're quiet do not wonder.
We are glad, so glad, yet ponder
On the loved ones left out yonder,
  Dundee's Own!

BULLET
Joseph Lee

Every bullet has its billet ;
　Many bullets more than one ;
God! Perhaps I killed a mother
　When I killed a mother's son.

TO JOSEPH LEE
William Johnston

Dear Joseph Lee, I'm glad tae see –
    Tho' times are no' sae rosy –
That ye hae still the he'rt an will
    Tae send us screeds o' poesy;
I'm blest if I – an' mair forbye –
    Can understand hoo ye
Can coort th' muse whaur Hell's let loose,
    An hunders daily dee.

Some sheltered nook beside a brook,
    Or 'neath a shady tree,
Is whaur I gang, when days are lang,
    Tae let my fancy flee;
While near at hand a feathered band
    Strikes up a melody,
Tae help my rhyme, an' a' the time
    Tae fill my he'rt wi' glee.

Sae, Joe, if I were sent oot bye
    To whaur you chance tae be,
I'm safe tae guess the printin' press
    Wad get nae poems frae me;
Th' first big shell that near me fell
    Wad scatter far an free,
If no' my brains, what there remains
    O' rhymin' art in me.

I pictured you, lad, tryin' tae woo
    The muse in you dug-oot,
Amid the hail o' shot an' shell,
    That maun be fleein' aboot;
Somehoo I think you'll hae tae juik
    Whene'er you hear a-comin'
A German shell, tae break the spell,
    An' set your lugs abummin'.

My wish is this – that they'll aye miss
    The poet frae auld Dundee,
That you'll come hame no' even lame,
    But wearin' a VC.
My blessin' true I send tae you,
    An' houp that day tae see,
When I will tak' a hearty shak'
    An' somethin' else wi' thee.

AUCTION
Brenda Shaw

The sale today
at Curr & Dewar's Auction Rooms
was the life work of a spinster
who painted in private,
didn't sell or exhibit.
Discouraged by critical friends, perhaps.

The local artists had heard
by word of mouth that
all her oil paints, brushes, water colours,
pastels, easels, palettes and carefully made
colouring boxes
lovingly collected and used over the years
would also be 'going for a song'.

They all came last night to the pre-sale view:
'The pictures are worthless,
but the frames are worth a bid.'
The entire Dundee art world
there to judge her total output,
appraising, shaking their heads:
'All that time and paint
over the years, and for what?
But they're beautifully framed!'
Her first and only private view.

And yet, there was the odd picture
I'd have been glad to have on my wall
(if it weren't already filled with my own
paintings, lovingly done but lacking genius):
a portrait of an old man,
face carved by wisdom and grief.
And a striking view at sunset across a field,
the shadows blue and long.
If I'd seen them in an exhibition
I'm sure I'd have thought them
better than most.

By the sale's end everything had gone,
down to the last brush.
She's maybe the only artist in the world
whose first exhibition
was a sell-out.

POLISH LASS, DUNDEE
Matthew Fitt

a draught o fremmit love
on each saft souch o braith,
Kamila Swecz in Overgate
redds the brod, spreads anither table cloot

this could be Bruges, Catania or Angers
but this howff's at Dundee
and that dern gliff in Kamila's neb
winna skail

hit's aiblins ainlie the aald toun's aynd
smittit yet wi Monck and Mone
reekit frae tally, jute and dragon's-blood,
the indelible imrie o the carline Jaffray
maskit five hunder year
ablow the burgh cundies
aizles aye flyin frae her raggit cloots like stars

but Kamila Swecz kens nae Grizzel
or the drouthie cronies at Stare Szkoty
or ocht o the banes o Kortykowski's sodgers
yirdit high on Balgay's braes

and Dundee
in its jizzen-bed o fire and ice
wha's ghaists and bairns aye cry hame
is no Kamila's acht

new cam til this caald airt,
hit's a love in a hoose on the Odra river,
a draught heavy wi femlie
and smeekit wi hersel
that kittles in Kamila's hert the day
blawn ben on the gates o Baltic winds
by Gdansk and Buddon Ness

STOBSWELL SET RADIO FUTURE
Richard Watt

All alive, repeat
Still alive if handle-less:
Patience could be the call sign
For the listening walls
The absence-thick air,
Our neighbour's cold finger
Trapped in his sideboard.

Were Plague into ham radio
She'd hear 'let them eat static'
Like Ricardo Montalban
Skateboarding down cobbled streets,
In a quest for the Tri-Force
And twenty B&H.

My walkman failed
And one grazed knee later
I took a test drive
From empty Struans Motors:
Oor Wullie and GPRS
Found no survivors.

So back to the CB;

Come in Winnipeg
Do I stand a chance?
PLEASE, THIS IS RODEO —
COME IN WINNIPEG.

THE UNPROVABLE FACT:
A TAYSIDE INVENTORY
John Burnside

I EXPLORERS

From a distance
   they only missed
what they never saw:
the pull of borderlines
   slow
tide shifts in the angle of a wall
the slip of water
   underneath a quay
shadows that came through snow
   on a journey home.
From a distance they began
   the stories they would use
as camouflage:
ghost companions
   birds beneath their feet
rockfalls
   or the memory of something
lukewarm:
   moths and pollen
hidden in the seams
   of wintered shirts
gardens laid out in rows
   like oyster beds
a house of silverfish
   beyond the docks
the doorway thick with steam
   and the heat from their bodies
forcing exotic plants
   from stones and loam:
lobelia
   nasturtium
         wintersweet
rhubarb and garlic

privet and night-scented stock
and somewhere behind it all
    the children they were
sailing through the dark
    on winter nights
to needle-falls and cream
    and the blood-fruit they prized
above all others:
    crimson
mythical.

II SURVEYORS

The angel bound
    and stilled
in Euclid or Fibonacci
    the unprovable
fact of the physical world
and data that exist
    beyond all doubt:
sunfish
    and blue-stemmed grasses
and tender
    improbable gold
of cottonwood
    the thoughts of others
music in the dark
    the ultrasound
of bats around a pool
continuous
    with sunlight on the firth
the streaming roads
    to Perth or Invercarse
birchwoods
    and miles of pasture in the rain
come to a vivid standstill.
The fact of endurance
    decay
and the fact

of weathering
flakes of enamel
    a splinter of broken hull
gulls flickering at the shoreline
    year after year.
Nothing has been revealed
    or hidden
and yet the tide
    in certain weathers
raises these slow
    dank angels
from the sea
    and makes them visible:
a length of hemp
    a ravelled wing of oil.

III MEDICINERS

So much between healing
    and mending
a lame horse cured
    with oil and wintergreen
or treacle in the oats
    to ease a cough
though mostly
    it's the tenderness between
a drayman's hands
the heat
    in a shepherd's fingers
stills the wound
and strange things come
    to those who live
by water:
fishers with cold in their veins
or lines of salt
along the windward seams
of mended bones
so much still to learn
    of medicine

agar or silver for wounds
 the lucid dreams
of phosphorus
 a room
of fruits in embryo
 the weight
of silences and waking
 potash
settled in tinted jars
 and dusted tubers
wrapped in a film
 of sulphur
and it is the wind
 or rainstorms
or the sea
 repairs a soul
or is it magnetic north
 that brings us true
knitting the cut flesh
 smoothing the creases
in dreams?

IV HUSBANDMEN

The medieval lull
 of inland farms
that feeling
 a man will have
as he turns from work
 and crosses a yard
the sudden awareness of heat
 or the smell of malt
from miles away
 whatever it is that remains
in the hair or the bones
 or folded inside the ribcage
like a prayer
 that sense of a blessed self
beneath the skin

is here
in this summer noon:
    blisters of moss
and stonecrop
    on a wall
walking shadows
    blood-heat in the veins
and hanging on tented sticks
    above the crop
these hapless birds
– part-crow
part-Hieronymus Bosch –
the bodies falling
    dripping from the twine
like tallow
    or fat
and something in the wing
    that almost
flexes against your passing.
Primitive
    as nothing else has been
for centuries
    spilt
barley
    or the necessary stain
of sacrifice
    this breeding calm
this gaze of meat
    and bone.

LIZ MCCOLGAN
Matthew Fitt

like the city o braes,
she faced a caald wind

a shilpit lass
wi steel in her banes,
she saftened the thrawn backs
o the Sidlees and the Rockies
wi a million dour dawn trainin runs

and fae the caaed-oot hert o Haakhill
the lass traachled throu
tae the circles o siller and gowd
at Seoul and Barcelona

but like the toun
that helped her finn her feet,
she won nae kind reviews

the lass aye pit her fit tae the road
lined wi sair and greetin faces

she ayewis chose the steyest brae

for her
there wis ainlie the track
and gaein doon it –
hirplin or fleein –
but gaein doon it

yet atween her and the road
the sherp thin wind
and the sweirness o the world
is nae mair
nor a stane in her shoe

HAMISH
Michael Marra

Up at Tannadice
Framed in woodwork cool as ice
Keeping out the wolves in his particular way
A smile and a wave, a miraculous save they say,
Out runs Hamish and the ball's in Invergowrie Bay.

Up at Tannadice as they gently terrorise
Call the sentry, Oh Hamish give us a song
Raising the voices as high as the bridge is long
Nasser said hello and did you miss him while
      his voice was gone.

I remember that time, it was an evening game
A European tie in the howling rain
Gus Foy pointed to the side of the goal
And said
'There's Grace Kelly by Taylor Brother's coal'
In Tannadice.

Up at Tannadice
Watching as the fortunes rise
Smiling when he hears 'Ah it's only a game,
Win lose or draw you get home to your bed
    just the same'
But Hamish stokes young men's dreams into a
    burning flame.

SOUR JEWEL
i.m. Billy MacKenzie
Andy Jackson

I think it was the bustle of the place
that did for me, the record shop
oblivious, impersonal, that voice
above the local noise, here a joyful skip

and swoop, there the grating edge of teeth.
Billy's gone I heard. *The stupid sod
has done it*. No doubting such a truth
when all you knew of him said

this was how he'd always meant to go.
Surely he was asking for it, crooning
Gloomy Sunday down at Fat Sam's, grey
clouds round the baby grand, brewing

retribution in the belly of a double bass.
He'd done the city thing, there and back,
and back again. He left behind the house
he'd never known, the loaded deck

that dealt him aces, all of which he'd fold.
Somewhere there must be that feral
out-take from the studio, the wild
and lonely *dies irae* sung as a recessional,

his steep falsetto rise let off the leash,
foreshortened by the accidental melting
of the precious piece of vinyl, out of reach,
a limited edition, perhaps the only pressing.

A LAMENT FOR BILLY MACKENZIE
W. N. Herbert

The stranger in our city's voice is dead
so keep all Dundee silent for a day,
sheathe all your spoons within their mourning cases,
fling all your florins in devalued Tay:
let every mirror hold his fourteen faces,
    our strangest voice is dead.
Our angel of the ragcart and the river,
the patron saint of tinkies, whose gold lips
could loose euphoric shrieks that split our hips –
but now he's fallen out with song forever.

He opened up the kitschy shop that lies
down crooning in our crypt-like retro hearts:
he saw the gloom in Vitriola Sundays,
the glamour of the wide-boy turning martyr,
of being but not reaching Number One –
    let lessers eat those pies.
Praise chance that once delivered that voice here,
those gorgeous tonsils, that deranging larynx:
here electronica met its finest syrinx,
but now he's broke the glass that rang so clear.

From the Hilltown to the Hilton by white car,
he sped through squalls of gull-skriek blues
and autobahned it all the way to Perth,
or spued five pernods with blackcurrant juice
projectile-style at his career's birth
    back in the Ballinard.
Cross-breeding krautrock with hick cabaret
he reared his whippet-wild songs on a diet
of lonely sardines, teaching them to shit
on dollar-deafened executives' parquet.

Praise to that voice, which spans the octaves as
the roadbridge spans the river's range of tides
and snell winds, bullies of Siberia.
It holds the spheres together as they gride
and squeal, that mile-wide voice, in theory our
    town's diapase, ya bass.
His gypsy holler was holy jabber-code,
our Bowie of Baldovan Terrace: hark
to Billy, Bacharach of Baxter Park.
He was the Shirley Bassey of Bonnybank Road.

He was a runaway from glassing bores,
from gnashing fathers and the ties that blind:
he married in the pyramids of Vegas
some great American bra like Hughes designed,
then took off from the girl and grew oblique as
    fear dripped from every pore.
He lost his passport, filled guitars with piss,
or caught the look he called Swiss Eye when forced
to board a plane; he endlessly divorced
his old associate: certain success.

When sales were gone, and he'd gone through the friends,
the cash and contracts like a fine tilth streams
through a riddle (money's constant, we're what flows
to deadened chore or jagged crown), news came
of Lily's cancer: when your mother goes
    childhood likes to end.
But Billy was another person from
himself – if songs are mirrors then that voice
that could sing through him seemed to eye its choices,
no longer wanting to belong to him.

Lament now for the father who must touch
a cheekbone in the barn at Auchterhouse,
who knows it in the darkness and knows why
it is so cold. Duveted in overdose,
a photo album, dumbed at thirty nine –
    lament for that numb touch.

Lament the kind of silence in that shed,
the absence of all further variation
on that one breathing theme thieved from creation:
lament MacKenzie's lovely son is dead.

Lament and flood our gritty city please:
let no more pearls form in its greedy bite
to be flung in the Tay's unhearing glass.
Dissolved, he rises like an opposite,
the Catholic in all Calvinists, the lass
    within the laddie's ease.
Lorca would know this spirit: his hair, planted
now in Balgay, sends up *duende's* shoots.
His jawline was perfect. Let my tongue find its root in
this town's most joyous voice, its most lamented.

GLENDALE & CO. (EXCERPTS)
(After Walt Whitman)
James Geddes

The firm of Glendale & Co. —
    A Firm of undoubted respectability,
Its name honoured on the Exchange,
Its bills eagerly sought after, readily discounted,
Its ramifications extensive, its agencies scattered throughout
    the globe.

Once on a time the Firm small and unimportant,
It has grown great from small beginnings;
Now its factories cover acres of ground,
They have streets running through them;
They are a city in themselves.
The buildings palatial and mammoth,
No way showy, built for endurance;
Its chimneys tall like Egyptian obelisks;
The clock towers aspiring also —
Lit up at night, the discs flare like angry eyes in watchful
    supervision, impressing on the minds of the workers the
    necessity of improving the hours and minutes purchased
    by Glendale & Co.

The Firm dominated the Town, it is in a sense ubiquitous;
    it pervades it.
The workers are thousands strong:
Every morning a city-full of men, women, and children
    march through its portals;
Every meal-hour they are disgorged,
The Town always in excitement, stir, hubbub, commotion;
The call-boys clatter at early five;
The bells clang, the whistles shriek at regular intervals —
The workers—slaves of the ring, hurrying to and fro in
    obedience to summons —
The patter of their feet like the tread of an army;
There is a constant jostling and rumbling of lorries,
A tremendous throbbing of beams and pistons,

An incessant rattle of looms.

The atmosphere permeated with dust,

The faces of the people engrained with dirt and grime,

Their voices husky with the fluff settled on the throat and
    lungs —

It is questionable indeed if the townspeople have any real
    personal identity at all;

If they are not really themselves part and parcel a product of
    Glendale & Co.;

Questionable if its fluff is not also on their souls, if the
    interests of the great Firm have not dimmed their mental
    vision, and clouded their moral perceptions.

At night the Firm still predominant, still supreme,

The flame of its foundry blasts reflected on the heavens,
    casting a ruddy radiance as far as the confusion of stars
    in the Milky Way.

Glendale is a man of domestic habits.

His home apart from the town, standing secure from observa-
    tion, in the quiet of the suburbs;

Round it high walls and tall ancestral trees —

The latter the abode of a colony of rooks

(Rooks, true conservatives—no lovers of newness).

Din of the town not heard here, or only heard in a far-off
    subdued hum, adding to the prevailing sense of repose.

Town seen in its picturesque aspects only;

Seen the tall chimneys, the spires of the churches and
    hospitals,

Between them the haze ; over them the glamour of distance;

Not seen the dingy alleys, the filthy closes.

Extensive landscape, sea-scape: —

A serenity as of Heaven.

The broad river still in summer as a Highland lake,

The sailing vessels slow gliding,

The little boats tacking and re-tacking,

The paddle and screw steamers churning the waters, leaving
    in the air serpentine trails of smoke,

The seagulls, flecks of white, skimming the river's surface, or

sailing through the blue of the sky;
The broad opening estuary,
The venerable castle, keeping up a brave show of strength
and defiance —
The fashionable suburb sunning itself under its protection,
The long stretch of sand bar,
The white coombs of the waves breaking on the bar,
The guiding lighthouses.
The gardens and vineries of spacious extent;
The product, vegetable and fruits in their season.
Inside the house, ease, culture, comfort, refinement,
Pictures, some of them Scriptural, 'The Rich Man and
Lazarus', 'The Descent from the Cross', 'The Light
of the World';
The library well stocked; Carlyle, Ruskin, Emerson, in
evidence.
(The prophets no longer stoned or deposited in splendid
sepulchres —
Their works immured in morocco editions, reviewed in the
magazines, daintly talked of in the drawing-rooms:
Glendale, I warn you in passing, these writers are more
dangerous to you and your order than an army of
dynamitards).

The home of the workers,
Some of them two or three roomed, comfortable enough;
Some of them—abodes of the lowest—miserable dens.
A sample picture of the slums —
A conspicuous building towering above its neighbours,
A Babel Tower, with its ten flats divided into single rooms;
Entrance dingy, dark, discoloured,
Stairs unclean, the sinks in the passages sending forth
unpleasant effluvia,
Plaster broken streaming with moisture;
Scarcely a whole pane in the windows—newspapers battered
up in place of panes;
Tall chimneys in the neighbouring vomiting forth smoke
and soot,

Mill ponds sending forth oily, noxious exhalations.
The inhabitants—hereditary helots —
Low-browed, ugly, forbidding,
Grown-up gutter children—producers themselves of gutter
    children,
Rum drinkers, fiery, quarrelsome.
The disorder, confusion of Tophet;
Frequent there the brawl, the brutal assault, the shrieks and
    yells of murder,
Robbery, prostitution, vice;
Troublesome quarters for the police.
The rents gathered weekly—the key left in the door as an
    indication of bankruptcy when the dweller decamps.
Not unkind to each other, the inhabitants, in cases of dis-
    tress.
What have you to do with all this, Glendale?
Did you not pay them their penny a day?

Yet listen a moment, Glendale, of Glendale & Co.
I have been brooding over these things,
I have been thinking over your perfect automatical penny-in-
    the-slot system; over your home in the suburbs; over
    these dens in the slums —
The conclusion? That you are not such a practical man as
    you deem yourself to be, or as others deem you to be;
That in spite of the Scriptures we can only think of you as
    Raca—a fool.
Do you deem that such a state of matters can continue?
Glendale, you are the man that has built his house upon the
    sand:
Assuredly the flood will come, if not in your day, at least in
    the day of your successors.
Glendale ! there is a spiritual law of supply and demand
    which is higher than the law of the economists:
The demand of that law is that your relationship with your
    workers shall be human and sympathetic.
You cannot get rid of your obligation by appealing to the
    necessity of securing cheap labour, to compete with the
    foreigner.

You use men and women as machines at the peril of yourself;
    to the danger of society:
The demand of that law will not be evaded;
It will be paid in some fashion or another —
God's books always balance;
For the neglect of your workers you have the slums and its
    consequent miseries;
Your attention to your workers would be as certainly repaid
    with blessings.

Glendale! I think I saw you the other day;
It was at a meeting to greet a Distinguished Traveller.
Distinguished Traveller had penetrated to the heart of Africa.
The natives not acquainted with the blessings of civilisation,
    of trade, and of commerce,
Went naked, or nearly so, lived in huts in the forest, wore
    rings in their noses —
Unhappy benighted natives!
Natives not so anxious to receive the blessings of civilisation
    as could be wished, opposed the progress of Distinguished
    Traveller;
Some of them had to be hanged, some of them had to be
    shot —
Action of Intrepid Traveller quite justifiable in your eyes —
I saw you and others applauding him as spoke in his own
    justification:
It was necessary to impress on the mind of the natives the
    wholesomeness of discipline.
Natives idolatrous, worshippers of wooden gods;
Distinguished Traveller of a religious turn of mind—this also
    highly satisfactory:
In a moment of dire distress he cried unto Heaven—he
    informed the Supreme that if he were relieved he would
    mentioned the fact in the newspapers —
(Great concession this on the part of Distinguished Traveller
    —not always inclined to share publicity with any one).
Distinguished Traveller was relieved; strictly faithful to his
    word he mentioned the fact in the newspapers.

For these things—for his devotion to commerce, for his
courteous recognition of religion!—you honoured and
hurrahed him,
You bestowed upon him the freedom of the town.
Some day the projects and predictions of the Distinguished
Traveller will be carried out:
The native will become ashamed of his nakedness, he will no
more wear rings in his nose, he will quit his hut in the
forest,
He will give up his wooden gods, he will become as
enlightened in matters of religion as the Distinguished
Traveller;
For those things you will give the native the blessings of
civilisation—you will erect him slums like to those of
the Overgate and Scouringburn;
The slaver will no more carry away his children—they will
be brought up on the half-time system;
He will no longer eat his enemies; he will consume the
earnings of his children—the necessity for cheap labour
unfortunately not allowing you to employ himself.
Blessings on the valour, the enterprise of the Distinguished
Traveller!
Glendale, these are not looked upon as proper ideas ;
The Press neither encourages the ventilation of such doctrines
nor their promulgator;
It loves better the prophet and prophecy of smooth things.
The accepted doctrines —
That a State is eminently practical which looks after the
improvement of its breed of cattle;
That a State is in danger of becoming communistic which
looks after the condition of its toilers, which concerns
itself with the redemption of gutter children.
Have no alarm, Glendale!
You are eminently respected, you will continue to be respected,
You will receive in life the exceeding great reward of the
applause of blatant money-worshippers —
When your end draws nigh your high-feed physician will
becomes extremely anxious;
He will advise that your system needs toning up, generous

living, foreign travel, if your valuable life is to be
spared.

But, after all these things the end will come, and as certain
as the end will come adulatory sermons nearly sufficient
of themselves to waft you into Heaven.

5
THE TEMPER

THI MITHER TONGUE

Mark Thomson

Eh wiz boarn an bred in a toon called Dundee,
so wiz meh mither an fathir afore me.

Wiv got a habit o talking dead fest
we oor speech o which eh wiz blessed
thir ir sum that say it's a wee bit rah
well eh dinna think so ah tah.

Eh think it's brah,
it's fine an dandy, it's loose an free,
when eh talk in broad Dundee,
it's jist as meh fathir aye spoke ti me
fae eh wiz wee.

It's meh mither tongue, it's a weh o life
eh think thi talk wurse ower in Fife
they ah cha thi cud an talk like teuchters
an thi ither half, there ah poofters.

Well em fae Dundee, an proud ti be
wiv got sum dodgy sayins – el gee yi that,
but thir no that bad ti thi Dundee ear,
it's ah they outsiders that think it's queer.

Well em seek sair
we thi Dundee tongue bein brought doon.

That's how em here thi day,
ti put yiz straight,
eh love talking loose an free
when eh talk in broad Dundee.

It's whar em fae,
it's meh identity.
It's fae thi hert
eh share it we meh mither
meh fathir, meh brither

An ah thi fowk eh ken
we nae airs or graces
as eh go aboot an talk
ti Dundee Faces.

FRIDA KAHLO'S VISIT
TO THE TAY BRIDGE BAR
Michael Marra

We were all flooded with a scarlet light
It came through the window with the rain outside
All went quiet and a vision appeared
With a rose in her hair and a ring in her ear.

And she says, 'Buenos Dias boys this looks like the place
To make my re entry to the human race
Here I am and here I'll stay
Till it's Hasta La Vista and I'm on my way'.

And Vince says, 'She was a woman to whom life had been cruel'
And she lived with a fat man of the naïve school
He liked his beer and he put it about
But she truly loved him till the lights went out.

Then she made her way up to the Pearly Gates
She saw Saint Peter, he was pumping weights
He says, 'Hitch a lift upon this falling star
And make your way down to the Tay Bridge Bar'.

There'll be no more lies and no more tears
No more listening through the fat man's ears
No more tears and no more lies
No more looking through the fat man's eyes.

She said she'd never felt so happy in a long, long time
Her mind was relaxed and her body felt fine
She said, 'Put on Perdido', tonight's the night
I want to dance with Jimmy Howie in the pale moonlight'.

There'll be no more lies and no more tears
No more listening through the fat man's ears
No more tears and no more lies
No more looking through the fat man's eyes
We were all flooded with a scarlet light.

FLYING LESSONS

Ellie McDonald

Back an forrit atween the turrets o the Central Library
a wheen o halliket herrin gulls gae soopin an skreichin
wi a din like tae wauk the deid. Their littluns, teeterin
alang the ledges, watch fair bumbazed, as grown-ups
jouk an weave an tummle catmaa through the air.
Tak tent, tak tent, nae second chancies here,
nae canny rocks tae divie aff, nae seaweed slides
tae safety. Ye'll only need tae heiter aince
an doun ye'll blatter on the tap o Rabbie's heid.
But gin ye think life's easier for me,
tak a bit keek owre. That's me, joukin atween thae
double deck buses, wishin tae hell I had wings.

THERE WAS AN OLD MAN OF DUNDEE
Edward Lear

There was an Old Man of Dundee,
Who frequented the top of a tree;
When disturbed by the crows,
He abruptly arose,
And exclaimed, 'I'll return to Dundee.'

SAINLESS
Douglas Young

I hae stuid an hour o the lown midsimmer nicht
til twal o the knock i the leelang glamarie-licht
by the cherry-tree at the midden, luikan aa round.
There's never a steer owreby at the ferm-toun,
the reek gangs straucht i the luift, that's lither and gray,
wi an auntran gair o gowd i the North by the Tay.
The whyte muin owre Drumcarrow, the Lomond shawan
purpie i the West, and a lane wheep caaan.

The ither birds are duin, but thon whaup's aye busy,
wi the dirlan bubble-note that maks ye dizzy,
the daft cratur's in luve, tho it's late i the year,
aa round Lucklaw he's fleean wi an unco steer.
There's a wheen stots owre i the park by the mansion-hous,
skemblan about whiles, dozent and douce,
and a rabbit nibbles amang our raspberry canes
for aa our wire and our traps and the lave o our pains.

But the feck o the hour I hae gowpit owre the dyke,
taen up wi a sicht thonder that I dinna like,
a day-auld cowt liggan doun i the gress
and the Clydesdale mear standan there motionless.
The hale hour she has made never a steer,
but stuid wi her head forrit, rigid wi fear,
it's a wonder onie beast can haud sae still.
The fermer douts the cowt has the joint-ill,
that canna be sained. Ye'd speir gin his mither kens?
Ay, beasts hae their tragedies as sair as men's.

AT THE WELLGATE

Sean O'Brien

Their speechless cries left hanging in the cold
As human fog, as auditory stench,
The boreal flaneurs donate their stains
And thick cirrhotic sherries to the bench
Outside the precinct where they're not allowed,
And finding they've no stories to tell
And thus no purchase on the Christmas crowd,
Descend by means of manholes into Hell.

Which in their case is arctic and unmapped,
Its every inch the coiling thick of it,
As if the Piranesi of the tubes
Had framed a labyrinth of frozen shit,
In which they wander howling and rehearse
The notion that elsewhere could still be worse.

FUNERAL BY THE TAY

Andy Jackson

Labouring like farmers with his corpse,
unwieldy as potatoes in a sack,
we march him on his palanquin
along the shining path, pausing at kerbs,
waiting for the green man to flash.

Cars slow, offer a petition of horns
as smoke blows from the eastern ghats
of Tayport, holy dormitory town, thin
of streets and grey of walls, undisturbed
by grief beneath its shallow patina of ash.

Menfolk wait for us along the shore,
nervous as they chatter, offering to light
each others' cigarettes, trying not to laugh
too loud at muttered jokes. Eyes dim,
the procession stops, faces set like rock.

We settle him upon the pyre, a little Law
of walking sticks, umbrellas, last night's
copies of the Dundee Evening Telegraph.
The fire is lit, but no-one waits for him
to burn; we walk away, not looking back.

The burden of his body is behind him now,
but he has parcelled up his dowdy soul
for us, a dubious ornament bequeathed
in devilment. I picture him, a gallus shade
tapping minor deities for twenty quid.

The peculiar light of his dharma is a glow
you will not see for long. He leaves a hole,
as does the drawing of a needle from a sheath
of skin. The man he thought he was will fade,
and leave behind the things he never did.

THE CATALOGUE OF SHIPS
Robert Crawford

The Dundee Homeric Society appeals for sponsors,
Ignoring its own oral epic

Jammed out by jute-barons and soft-focus journos
Writing their PR Dundoniad

Through whose sieve the undiscovered
Pour down – a firth that shines like India,

Sharp as the Archangel snows –
Every person a kind of vessel

History does not list:
The dissector's cousin clutching her small leather bag

While the Ferry Road floods with elephant,
The unshod, the filthy-shoed, councillors coughing and nudging,

Arctic footballers, bridge-rebuilders,
The Submarine Miners' Brass Band:

Everyone here is ordinary,
Silvery, hard-faced, bonnie.

FURNISHINGS IN A DUNDEE PUB
Ian Cadman

these stools are amazing
cast iron
you can hardly lift them
that was maybe
the idea.

HOOSE PROOD
Mary Brooksbank

Here lies puir Jess in her last rest,
    She had nae life worth bummin',
Nae ploys, nae lauchs, nae fun or jest,
    Jess died the perfect woman.

For Jessie never made a mistake,
    Her hoose was aye in order,
She never wi' her neebors claiked,
    And bairns and gods abhorred her.

For chasin' every speck of dirt,
    Jess never took a minute;
And noo tae think, whit maks it hurt,
    The craiter's happit in it.

45, ARK ROAD (PARK ROAD)
Richard Watt

A lamplighter whistles in the street
grinning at a half-done day.

Clouds speak in strong brogues
and hail begins to hobble down her way.

Where the lintel meets the corner of her room
pockets bend and bow, as rivers run along.

Brown, tea-stained water fills the mugs
and tributary cups they run into.

She delights at wet shelves and receipts
even as the bed sheets soak right through:

Every spoon's a suitor in the sagging drawer
entreating laughter with their ribald songs.

VALENTINE
Judith Taylor

Meet me near the clock
at the top of the Wellgate.
Meet me just before mid-day

and you will see
as we stand there talking
how the whole machinery opens

into motion;
birds, bells,
a song.

Everything stops a moment
for its everyday serenade.

And it could happen
for you and me,
love. So what do you say?

We only have to find the right time
and be there.

ON ANN STREET, FRIDAY NICHT
Ellie McDonald

Listen,
spray pentan the Mad Dog,
thrie wee fires an hauf a dizzen bricks
disnae constitute a riot.
An we wir hyne awaa
afore the polis hut the broken gless.

Our New Labour Councillor's beilin.
This is an arty-farty toun
o the parvenu an the nouveau riche,
an we're the keech they stood on.

Listen, poet,
only deid fish sweem wi the tide.
Get yersel a brick.

ON ANN STREET, SUNDAY MORNING
Ellie McDonald

Ye cudnae tell hou auld the Mini wis,
its burnt out shell abandoned at the cribbie.
A Dundee double whammy:
Setterday nicht joyride an boney.

I'd missed it aa – the polis, the firies,
an the smack-heid up abune the shop
bungan tins o pent intae the street.

We're 'learning a sense of community' here,
sae naebody clyped tae the polis.
But Kippy's a braw wee drehver
fur a ten year auld.

ADDENDA

Don Paterson

(i)
The Gellyburn is six feet under;
they sunk a pipe between its banks,
tricked it in and turfed it over.
We heard it rush from stank to stank,
Ardler Wood to the Caird Estate.

Scott said when you crossed the river
you saw sparks; if you ran at it
something snagged on the line of water.

(ii)
It was Scott who found the one loose knot
from the thousand dead eyes in the fence,
and inside, the tiny silver lochan
with lilies, green rushes, and four swans.
A true artist, he set his pitch:

uncorking the little show for tuppence
he'd count a minute on his watch
while a boy set his eye to the light.

(iii)
One week he was early, and turned up
at the Foot Clinic in Kemback Street
to see a little girl parade
before the Indian doctor, stripped
down to just her underthings.

Now he dreams about her every night
working through his stretches: The Mermaid ;
The Swan; The Tightrope-Walker; Wings.

(iv)
They leave the party, arm in arm
to a smore so thick, her voice comes
to him as if from a small room;
their footprints in the creaking snow
the love-pact they affirm and reaffirm.

Open for fags, the blazing kiosk
crowns old Jock in asterisks.
He is a saint, and Scott tells him so.

HERMLESS
Michael Marra

Wi' ma hand on ma hert and ma hert in ma mooth
Wi' erms that could reach ower the sea,
Ma feet micht be big but the insects are safe
They'll never get stood on by me.
Hermless, hermless, there's never nae bother fae me-
I ging to the libry, I tak' oot a book
And then I go hame for ma tea.

I save a' the coupons that come wi' the soup
And when I have saved fifty-three,
I send awa fifty, pit three in the drar,
And something gets posted tae me.
Hermless, hermless, there's never nae bother fae me-
I dae whit I'm telt and I tidy my room
And then I come doon for my tea.

There's ane or twa lads wha I could cry my chums
They're canny and meek as can be
There's Tam wi' his pigeons, and Wull wi' his mice,
And Robert McLennan and me.
Hermless, hermless, there's never nae bother fae me-
I ging to the libry, I tak' oot a book
And then I go hame for ma tea.

Hermless, hermless, there's never nae bother fae me-
Naebody'd notice that I wasnae there
If I didnae come hame for ma tea.

DUNDEE HOSPITAL WARD
Tom Scott

Ay, whiles I think on thir auld bits and banes,
The cancered, rottit, syphilitic anes
Liggan yonder, waitin for mercifu death
To come and take awa their last, tormentit braeth
And lat them be for aa the lave o time.
They glowered on me as gif it were a crime
To be tortured by life, and no daeth, like them.
Whaur did they hail frae? Whitna kin' o hame
Wes left in whit kin' o state to byde their en'?
In whitna Dundee dunnie did some auld hen
Sit at her open windae aa her lane –
Lookin doun on some waste-littert street
Whaur raggit weans wi waesome bare feet
Play like mongrels in the clairty gutters,
Or speil up lamp-posts or chip-shop shutters –
Spieran at ilka passan face for his, in vain?
Or in whit dowdie and genteel prefab
Did young things hope and pray that his grizzlet gab
Providence wad staw
Ance for aa?

THE HOUSE I NEVER LIVED IN
Pippa Little

not Forfar Road –
one ring, plug-in cooker
under my bed
as milk bottles of piss
multiply along the kitchen skirting

or Caird Avenue
where I turned invisible
among someone else's effects
blind and tongueless
last one of my kind

or Bellefield's
rainy green,
Thursday night baths down at the leisure centre,
crackled plastic armchairs for duets of
The Ballad of Matty Groves –

the house I never lived in
was there all the time
still with its fragrant name
in an unvisited part of town

so when I finally track you down,
family party in sunlight under bay windows,
Nurse in her whites and you in woollens,
a leafy and capacious breeze, the sounds of tennis,
your mother obscured by a paper parasol,

as I arrive from the future
deja vu makes me shivery,
I walk up Cedarlea's curled drive
wondering what time of day it is,

what if none of you know me?

UNTITLED

Syd Scroggie

The soot on the cassies,
    The drunk on the seat,
The jute on the lassies,
The fog in the street;
The gleam in the shutter,
    The smell of the fry,
The fag in the gutter,
    Unhappy am I.

The moss on the boulder,
The sun in the glen,
The cloud on the shoulder,
The snow on the ben;
The deer on the rigging,
    The lark in the sky,
A friend in the bigging,
    And happy am I.

11:00: BALDOVAN
Don Paterson

Base Camp. Horizontal sleet. Two small boys
have raised the steel flag of the 20 terminus:

me and Ross Mudie are going up the Hilltown
for the first time ever on our own.

I'm weighing up my spending power: the shillings,
tanners, black pennies, florins with bald kings,

the cold blazonry of a half-crown, threepenny bits
like thick cogs, making them chank together in my pockets.

I plan to buy comics,
sweeties, and magic tricks.

However, I am obscurely worried, as usual,
over matters of procedure, the protocol of travel,

and keep asking Ross the same questions:
where we should sit, when to pull the bell, even

if we have enough money for the fare,
whispering, Are ye sure? Are ye sure?

I cannot know the little good it will do me;
the bus will let us down in another country

with the wrong streets and streets that suddenly forget
their names at crossroads or in building-sites

and where no one will have heard of the sweets we ask for
and the man will shake the coins from our fists onto the counter

and call for his wife to come through, come through and see this
and if we ever make it home again, the bus

228

will draw into the charred wreck of itself
and we will enter the land at the point we left off

only our voices sound funny and all the houses are gone
and the rain tastes like kelly and black waves fold in

very slowly at the foot of Macalpine Road
and our sisters and mothers are fifty years dead.

TILL FORTUNE TURNS THE WHEEL

Mary Brooksbank

There's a laddie in this toon,
  'Twas him brocht me tae shame,
For when misfortune frowned on me
  He denied he kent my name.
But wi' my bairnie on my knee,
  I'll kiss it and wish him weel,
And maybe he'll get time tae think,
        When Fortune turns the wheel.

Oh, mony's the sair, sair he'rt I've haen,
  Jist like tae brak in twa;
Mony's the sair, sair feet I've ta'en
  Gaen thro' the frost and snaw;
I've wrocht hard in mill and field,
  Tae earn my every meal,
But maybe I'll get some happiness yet,
        When Fortune turns the wheel.

Oh, weel I mind that sad, sad, day,
  The day my mither de'ed;
She placed her hand in mine tae say,
  Lassie, dear, tak' heed,
Ye'll hae fause freens wha'll flatter you
  While your good name they steal,
But 'Dree yer weird' whar ere ye be,
        Till Fortune turns the wheel.

Here's tae my pretended freens,
  Here's tae ye ane and a',
Although ye turned yer backs on me
  When mine was tae the wa';
But wi' a full gless in my hand,
  I'll drink and wish ye weel,
Wi' as warm a he'rt, but wiser head,
        Till Fortune turns the wheel.

There's days I sing sae cheery,
    For a' that's come tae me;
There's time I feel sae weary
    I could lay me doon tae dee;
But still I'll no let doon my he'rt,
    I've steeper braes tae speil,
Wi health and strength I'll breist them a'
      Till Fortune turns the wheel.

QUHO IS AT MY WINDO?

John Wedderburn

Quho is at my windo, quho, quho?
Go from my windo, go, go.
Quha callis thair, sa lyke ane stranger,
   Go from my windo, go.

Lord I am heir, ane wratcheit mortall,
That for Thy mercy dois cry and call,
Unto The, my Lord Celestiall,
   Se quho is at my windo, quho.

How dar thow for mercy cry?
Sa lang in sin as thow dois ly,
Mercy to haif thow art not worthy,
   Go from my windo, go.

My gylt, gude Lord, I will refuse,
And the wickit lyfe that I did use,
Traistand Thy mercy sall be myne excuse:
   Se quho is at thy windo, quho.

To be excusit, thow wald rycht faine,
On spending of thy lyfe in vaine,
Having my Gospell in greit disdaine,
   Go from my windo, go.

O Lord, I haif offendit The;
Excuse thairof thair can nane be,
I haif followit thamc that sa teichit me,
   Se quho is at thy windo, quho.

Nay, I call the nocht fra my dure, I wis,
Lyke ane stranger that unknawin is;
Thow art My brother, and My will it is,
   In at my dure that thow go.

With rycht humill hart, Lord, I the pray,
Thy confort and grace obtene I may,
Schaw me the path and reddy way
    In at Thy dure for to go.

I am cheif gyde to riche and pure,
Schawand the path way rycht to my dure,
I am their confort in everie hour,
    That in at my dure will go.

Bot thay that walk ane uther way,
As mony did teiche from day to day,
That were indurit, my Gospell did say,
    And far from my dure sall go.

O Gracious Lord, confort of all wicht,
For Thy greit power and excellent micht,
Sen Thou art cheif gyde, and verray licht,
    In at thy dure lat me go.

Man, I gaif the nocht fre will
That thow suld my Gospell spill;
Thow dois na gude bot ever ill,
    Thairfoir from my dure that thow go.

That will, allace! hes me begylit,
That will sa sair hes me defylit,
That will Thy presence hes me exilit;
    Yit in at Thy dure lat me go.

To blame that will thow dois not rycht;
I gaif the ressoun, quhairby thow mycht
Haif knawin the day by the dark nycht,
    In at my dure for to go.

Lord, I pray The with all my hart,
Of thy greit mercy remufe my smart;
Lat ane drop of Thy Grace be my part,
    That in at thy dure I may go.

I haif spokin in my Scripture:
I will the deide of na creature;
Quha will ask mercy sall be sure,
    And in at my dure for to go.

O Lord, quhais mercy is but end,
Quhairin ocht to The I did offend,
Grant me space my lyfe to amend,
    That in at Thy dure I may go.

Remember thy sin, and als my smart,
And als for the quhat was my part;
Remember the speir that thirlit my hart,
    And in at my dure thow sall go.

And it war yit till do againe,
Rather or thow suld ly in paine
I wald suffer mair in certane,
    That in at my dure thow mycht go.

I ask nathing of the, thairfoir,
Bot lufe for lufe to lay in stoir:
Gif me thy hart, I ask no moir,
    And in at my dure thow sall go.

O Gracious Lord Celestiall,
As Thow art Lord and King Eternall,
Grant us grace that we may enter all,
    And in at Thy dure for to go.

Quho is at my windo, quho?
Go from my windo, go;
Cry na mair thair, lyke ane stranger,
    Bot in at my dure thow go.

JUTE
Harvey Holton

In twistin yarns the present is biggit
in awe pairts o this toon: the hert an harns
o fowk are richt riggit tae ken its boon.
Icy the East wund in winters cauld nicht
blaws men hame frae whaur awe iles are fund
deep oot o sicht an taen wie the same game
in barrels rotund wie the deid an live fricht
that still isnae taem as the laust nettin grund:
sae wie knots the licht brek; the twists the same.
Unwinde the waves bobbin, let the kettle bile,
the weemin wark fur a sodgers unkent sobbin
in the auld style. See the seamless serk
in the derk continent throbbin the while
o the missions ark; the empires robbin
threidit tae the mile o the empy bark.
Fowk are richt riggit tae ken this boon,
in awe pairts o this toon the herts an harns
in twistin yarns o the present are biggit.

JUTE SPINNER
George Bruce

What is it makes that shuttle fly?
Not ultimately the stroke of an uninformed engine,
Nor the subtle project of a capital enterprise.

What is it makes that shuttle fly?
Not a high voltage,
Nor current transmitted from a central store,
But every strand woven,
Every strand forced in
Warp and weft
Moves in its intricacy
From her nerves and bones and blood.

THRIFT
Margaret Gillies Brown

In farmhouses, up and down the land,
when recession bites you return to
things your mother taught you,
country practices floating down the centuries.
Windows in the kitchen sweat
with steam from soup boiling in the pot.
Children wait for bits from the baking bowl
to make their own small tarts and cakes
then willingly hand you jar upon jar
of jam for the topmost shelf
to wait in legions of ruby and lighter reds.
Hungry men come in from the harvest fields,
say how good the kitchen smells.

On winter evenings
after the dogs are fed, the last dish washed,
you retreat to living rooms like this one
smelling of woodsmoke and geraniums
where your nearest has lit the stove,
drawn the crimson curtains.
You settle tired limbs
while from the glowing copper
he throws on wood that crackles and spits.
The room basks in warmth given at small cost.
The grandchild in your arms, one cheek sorely flushed,
falls asleep to your rocking
and you're faintly aware of the farmhouse crooning
old songs.

DUNDONIAN U.X.O.
Richard Watt

You mean well, and also death
To an uneasy shepherd lad
Beardless and big-planned

Out of the woods at Lethe
Skip across fields of U.X.O.
Over-watch imagined basilisks, trolls.

Silly thinks uranium
Only has a half-life
When you are not there.

Then he goes back into the mountains.

I see
Street lamps and packed snow
Still guide your journey home.
Black slipping ice, needling flechettes
Scrape every muscle:

Is it so
There's no dog to warm your bones
Or at the least
Mess up your hanging scarves
With needy, soaking hair;
No one else is alive
To pull through the safeless air –

Silence, an unwatched B-film
Mopes behind you,
Jostling for the attention
Of your watched eyes.

A DIHZEEZ CA'D DUNDONESE
Gary Robertson

Like that mythical place ca'd Brigadoon
Thirz a myth goin roond in Dundee toon
Thit wiv somehow cheenjed thi weh wi speak
Well itz gittin some fowk here pussay seeck
Eh, some lihterary nedz fae wir local press
Think thi ken thi gemme, think thit thay ken best
DUNDONESE! Hiv ye ivir heard thi like?
Iv heard o Chinese eh, but no this alien shite!

Now, mebbe thi Broonz an Oor Wullie speak like that
Half Inglish-pidgin-Brechin-cum-Serbo-Croat
But thare jist cartoonz in a book
Its obvious some writers dinna lissin or look
Or ken wutz goin on on this streetz
'Thi wurd on thi pavey' wi thi real fowk ye meet
Eh, yull no hear any Dundonese oot thare
Jist pure Dundonian – itz alehv an itz rare!

Sure, wi mibbee gibber pish wile hammirin thi swally
Speak Taiwanese, Lebanese an dialects fae Bali
Christ, yull mibbee even hear wi speak polite
Well mibbee no! An certainly no this Dundonese shite
Itz time thi perpetrators hung thir sorry hades in shame
Yir dealin wi oor culture – no some cool linguistic game
It wuzna then, it izna now, itz nivir gonna be
This language is Dundonian, an thatz thi weh it'll ayewiz be!

DUNDEE HEATWAVE

Sean O'Brien

The rotundas of the mercantile retired
Glint with speculation. Telescopes are aimed
Along the horizon sudden heat has blurred,
Where Fife habitually stands.
Low steamers slide beneath the bridge
For the remote interiors. Northern tropics
Sweat in the mind's eye and offer
Their opals and foot-rot and concubines
Round the next bend, or the next,
Or wherever young Hawkins and Hannay
Awake in their hammocks, alert
To the sshh of a dog-end of water.
That was the promise, think brittle old men,
Recapping the lenses and gingerly going
Downstairs to the papers and still afternoons
In the cool of their money, to study
The movements of shadows that reach
For their final disposal, the perfect just-so
That accounts for the rest, like a moral.
That was the promise, of stepping from shore
At the foot of the page, the beginning.

BIOGRAPHICAL NOTES

Blind Harry was thought to have lived from 1440-1492, and was a troubadour to the court of James IV. He is best known for his epic Scots poem *The Actes and Deidis of the Illustre and Vallyeant Campioun Schir William Wallace*, (often known simply as '*The Wallace*') which was written in about 1477. The poem was used as source material for the screenplay of the Hollywood movie 'Braveheart'.

James Adams was born and raised in Dundee. He has been writing since the early seventies, with poems published in magazines and anthologies both local and national. These include *New Writing Dundee* and *Gallimaufry*. He is a member of the Hillton and Dighty Connect Writing Groups, has three poems on a plinth in Hilltown Park, Dundee and has spoken at Edinburgh Book Festival and the Scottish Poetry Library.

Kate Armstrong was born in England in 1944 and grew up in the east of Scotland, moving to Dundee in 1969. She began writing in the 1980s. Her work has been published in a range of poetry magazines and anthologies in the UK and Europe. Her first collection appeared in 1993; her next, a dual language collection, is due in 2013. She contributed a Scots translation to the PEN international poem relay in 2008.

William Beharrie was born in Dundee in 1834. Beharrie's poetry is concerned with contemporary life in nineteenth century Dundee and surrounding area. Several of his poems were published in the local press and by all accounts were very popular. At the age of two, he nearly drowned in the lade of a Dundee spinning mill. He was sent to live with an aunt in the country where he was educated in the village school. He later worked in a Dundee hatters and as a wood turner. He married in 1854 and had four children. His short autobiography expresses regret at his youth misspent in Lochee. He died in 1890. William Beharrie is Dundee poet Matthew Fitt's great-great-great-grandfather.

Mary Brooksbank was born in Aberdeen in 1897, moving with her family to Dundee in 1907. Due to her political activity (including involvement in the 1921 Dundee riots) she spent three periods in prison, turning to poetry while imprisoned in Perth. Also a violinist and singer, her poetry and song lyrics were published together and for the first time in 1966. She died at Ninewells Hospital, Dundee, in 1978. Dundee's Brooksbank Library is named in her honour.

Margaret Gillies Brown is a poet and writer. Born near Edinburgh, she trained as a nurse at Dundee Royal Infirmary, gaining her S.R.N. in 1952. Living with her husband on various Perthshire farms, she has raised seven children and travelled extensively. Margaret has eight full-length poetry collections published and three works of biography and autobiography.

Forbes Browne is a poet and retired teacher. He writes with the Broughty Ferry Environmental Project Eco Poets group. He has contributed to two pamphlets by the Eco Poets, *Inspired by Nature* and *Stories Older than the World*, and has appeared in *Poetry Scotland* and *New Writing Scotland*. Poet W.N. Herbert and novelist James Meek are two of Forbes's former pupils.

George Bruce was born in Fraserburgh in 1909. Graduating from Aberdeen University, he taught English and History at Dundee High School. He produced programmes for BBC Radio Aberdeen and BBC television, including the first television arts programme in Scotland. He published eight collections of poetry and edited three Scottish anthologies. Bruce was awarded an OBE in 1984, and in 1999 – at the age of 90 – he won the Saltire Society's Scottish Book of the Year award for *Pursuit: poems 1986-1998*. He died in 2002.

Colette Bryce was born in Derry, Northern Ireland, in 1970. She lived in London until 2002, becoming Fellow in Creative Writing at the University of Dundee (2003-2005) and North East Literary Fellow at the University of Newcastle upon Tyne (2005-2007). She currently divides her time between London and Newcastle, working as a freelance teacher and editor. She has written five full-length poetry collections, including *Self-Portrait in the Dark* (2008).

John Burnside is a multi-award-winning poet and author. Born in Dunfermline in 1955, he is a former Writer in Residence at the University of Dundee, now teaching Creative Writing, Literature, and Ecology courses at St. Andrews University. He is one of only two poets to have won both the T.S. Eliot Prize and the Forward Poetry Prize for the same collection – *Black Cat Bone* (2011). Along with fifteen poetry collections, he has published eight novels and three works of non-fiction. His recent novel *The Mercy Boys (2000)* is set in Dundee.

Ian Cadman was born in Liverpool in 1959, and moved to Dundee aged 11. He attended Dundee High School then Dundee College of Technology. He began writing about 1981, and was a member of Dundee University Writers Group, and made many contributions to poetry magazines in the 1980s while resident in Perthshire. *Furnishings in a Dundee Pub* is taken from the magazine *Logos* (1982).

Athole Cameron was a poet, writer, playwright, and primary school teacher. Born in 1923, she trained at the Dundee College of Education and taught in various schools across Perthshire and Edinburgh before retiring in 1982. She was a member of the Scots Language Society, the Saltire Society, and the Scottish National Party, standing for Parliament three times and founding the party's Heritage Society. Along with her poetry, she wrote short stories and scripts: her play *The Eve of Saint Paul* is based on a true incident in 1544 when a woman was drowned in the Tay for witchcraft. *The Tartan Chameleon: selected writing of Athole Cameron* was published in 2005.

Donald Campbell is a poet, playwright, director, and theatre historian. Born in Caithness, he grew up in Edinburgh where he currently lives. Forming the community theatre company 'The Old Town Theatre' in the 1980s, he has gone on to write many stage plays and radio plays and has written two volumes of theatre history. His first five collections of poetry are represented in *Selected Poems: 1970–1990*, and *Homage to Rob Dunn* was published in 2007. Donald was awarded an Honorary Fellowship by the Association for Scottish Literary Studies in 2010.

George Colburn was born near Aberdeen in 1852. Training as a grocer, he worked as a Fruit Market Commission Agent in Glasgow. Married with four children, he died at his daughter's home in Glasgow in 1937, aged 84. A 'lost' poet, his work *Poems on Mankind and Nature* was rediscovered in a bookshop in Ayr in 2008.

Robert Crawford is a poet, scholar, and literary critic. Born in Lanarkshire in 1959, he is currently Professor of English at St. Andrews University. He has co-edited several poetry anthologies, including *The New Penguin Book of Scottish Verse* (2000), and with W.N. Herbert he co-authored *Sharawaggi: Poems in Scots* (1990). His own poetry has appeared in six full-length collections including *Full Volume* (2008) and *Talkies* (1992). He makes regular appearances at literary events in Dundee and was recently published in *New Writing Dundee* (2010).

Valerie Cuming was born in London, brought up in Havana. A member of the former Writers' Group sponsored by Dundee University and the Scottish Arts Council, she was helped by many of the Writers in Residence. Valerie writes mainly poems and short stories, and has been published in small magazines. She is a postal member of Perthshire Writers and contributes to 'A Pocketful of Perthshire' at the Annual Festival of the Arts. She belongs to Ver Poets and to Poetry for Joy which produces an annual anthology.

Robert Dallas was a poet, author, and translator. Born in Jamaica in 1754, he studied Law in England and there settled. He became friends with Lord Byron – his sister marrying Byron's uncle – and it is primarily for this reason he is remembered. It was by Dallas's advice that *Childe Harold* was published and, following Byron's death, he prepared his 'Recollections of Lord Byron', published posthumously. Among his writings are *Annals of the French Revolution* (1800), translated from the French of Bertrand de Moleville, and his novel *Aubery* (1804). He died in Normandy in 1824.

David Dick was a scientific researcher, teacher, and poet. Born in Glasgow in 1927 and graduating from Glasgow University, he held research and teaching posts in Oxford, Copenhagen, and North Carolina before being appointed Cox Professor of Anatomy at the University of Dundee. He was responsible for building up the distinguished Anatomy Department in the University's Medical Sciences Institute, which continues to be a world leader in anatomy and forensic science. Actively interested in politics, David became honorary vice-president of Dundee's Liberal Democrat Party, standing in the local council elections. He was forced to retire due to illness in 1991 and his poetry collection *Physics of the Heart* confronts his struggle with heart disease. He died in 1992.

C.B. Donald is a native Dundonian, born in 1968. He graduated from the University of Dundee in 2000 with a degree in English and Modern History. He is a member of the Nethergate Writers and has had short fiction published in their last three anthologies. This is his first published poetry.

Dylan Drummond was born in Perth, Scotland in 1969 but has lived in Dundee from childhood. He is a Dundee based filmmaker who produces and directs documentary for cinema and broadcast. He was official photographer for the Dalai Lama visit to Scotland in 2012. Dylan's films are both used at a local, educational level in schools, colleges and universities, at film festivals around the world and more recently by the BBC. He produced and directed a short film about literacy issues for the BBC in 2012 and in 2013 will create 3 films for the BBC about numeracy issues.

Douglas Dunn is a poet, scholar, and literary critic. Born in Renfrewshire in 1942, he gained degrees in librarianship and English literature before working in the Brynmor Jones Library under Philip Larkin. He was professor of English at St. Andrews University until retirement in 2008. His poetry was recently collected in *New Selected Poems 1964-2000*. He holds an honorary doctorate from the University of Dundee.

G.F. Dutton was a poet and scientist. Born in Chester in 1924, he earned a PhD in biochemistry from Edinburgh University before holding a research professorship at Queen's College, Dundee. His research led to the biochemistry department's international influence and reputation. A wildwater swimmer, mountain climber, piper, and forester, he published essays on his various passions and interests. He saw his first poetry collection, *Camp One*, published when he was aged 54, three further collections appearing before his death aged 85.

Norrie Elder was born in Dundee in 1948. He worked in Dundee jute mills, on oil rigs in the Gulf of Mexico, as a dock watchman and dry-stone dyker, and had lived in Greece and London. Norrie's favourite writers were Heine, Rilke, Pessoa and Nash. He had met Ginsberg and drunk whisky with Norman MacCaig, whose poetry he admired. Though poetry was his life, he made little effort to get his poems published, although some appeared in *Aquarius*, *Scotia Review*, *Gallimaufry*, *Logos*, and *Riverrun* magazines. An affectionate portrait of him, only loosely fictionalised as 'Atholl Graham', appears in Andrew Murray Scott's novel *Tumulus*. He died in 2008 at the age of 59.

Raymond Falconer trained in the Department of Printing at Duncan of Jordanstone College of Art, Dundee, and has worked as a printer. His poems have been published in *Akros, Effie, Open Space*, and in the anthology *Four Scottish Poets* (1983).

Matthew Fitt was born in Dundee in 1968 and now lives in Prague. He was Brownsbank Writing Fellow from 1995 – 1997 and Writer in Residence for Greater Pollok in Glasgow in 2001. He is the author of the first sci-fi novel written in Scots *But n Ben A-Go-Go* (2000) and poetry collection *Kate o Shanter's Tale* (2003). His history of Dundee for children *Time Tram Dundee* (2006) was distributed to all the city's schools. He is co-founder of the award-winning Itchy Coo Scots language imprint. From 2001 – 2011, he was National Scots Language Development Officer working in every community in Scotland and presenting the case for Scots at the United Nations.

A.D. Foote was born in Manchester and attended Balliol College, Oxford. Depressive illness interposed and he lived in various places before settling in Dundee in 1969, often referring to himself as a 'West European'. He was at one time a translator in Esperanto. His poetry appeared in *AMF*, *Gallimaufry*, and *Words Magazine*, and a booklet of his poems, *The House in Not Right in the Head*, was published by local publishers Blind Serpent in 1986, for which Douglas Dunn contributed a foreword. He was a member of the University of Dundee's Writers' Workshop. He died in 1996 at the age of 65.

Bashabi Fraser is a poet, writer, and academic. Born in India and now based in Edinburgh, her teaching, research, and writing reflect her interest in the transnational and transcultural, combining her eastern heritage and western experience. She holds degrees from Calcutta University and Edinburgh University and teaches at several universities in India and Scotland. Bashabi won the AIO Award for Literary Services in 2009 and was a Finalist for the Women Empowered Award for Art and Culture in Scotland. Her modern epic poem *From the Ganga to the Tay*, forming a conversation between the two rivers, was published in 2009.

David Fyans was born in 1979. He studied Time Based Art at Duncan of Jordanstone College of Art & Design where he is currently undertaking a Masters in Fine Arts. His practice revolves around subconscious interventions, mysticism, psychogeography, extra-dimensional and liminal spaces and ruminations on time and our relationship with it.

James Young Geddes was born in Dundee in 1850. He traded as a tailor in the city before moving to Alyth in the 1880s, where he continued his business and served for some time as a baillie. He published his first collection of poetry, *The New Jerusalem*, in 1879 while still in Dundee, followed later by *The Spectre Clock of Alyth and other Selections* and *In the Valhalla and other Poems*. A member of the Alyth Literary Society, he was also an artist, some of his paintings remaining on display today in Alyth town buildings. He died in Alyth in 1913.

Valerie Gillies was born in Canada in 1948 and grew up in southern Scotland. She was the second 'Edinburgh Makar' or poet laureate of the city, 2005-2008 – an ancient office reinstated in 2002. She is the author of nine collections of poetry, including *The Spring Teller* (2002), and regularly collaborates with other artists, including illustrators, photographers, harpists, textile artists, book makers, and sculptors. Writing her first poems at Edinburgh University under Norman MacCaig, she has earned the name 'the river poet' after following both the Tweed and the Tay from source to sea.

John Glenday was born in Broughty Ferry, Dundee, in 1952. He graduated as a psychiatric nurse and worked in Dundee for many years before being appointed the Scottish/Canadian Exchange Fellow at the University of Alberta, where he taught at the Banff Centre. His poetry has been widely published and acclaimed. He has been awarded the XE Nathan Prize, the Scottish Arts Council Book Prize for *The Apple Ghost* (1989), a Poetry Book Society Recommendation for both *Undark* (1995) and *Grain* (2009), and has been shortlisted for both the Griffin Poetry Prize 2010 and the Ted Hughes Award for Excellence in New Poetry 2010.

W.N. Herbert has published eight volumes of poetry and five pamphlets. He is Professor of Poetry and Creative Writing in the School of English at Newcastle University. Recent publications include *Omnesia* (Bloodaxe, 2013), and *Murder Bear* (Donut Press, 2013). He has translated poetry from Bulgarian, Chinese, Farsi, Somali and Turkish. Along with Yang Lian, he edited *Jade Ladder* (Bloodaxe, 2012), an anthology of contemporary Chinese poetry.

Harvey Holton was born in Galashiels in 1949. Growing up between Nigeria, Edinburgh, Falkirk, and Lambert, he settled and married in Fife in 1971, attending the University of Dundee. Graduating with Honours in English Literature, he worked for several years as a forester in Fife, Perthshire, and the Borders. Meeting considerable success with his poem *Finn* (1987), an innovative poem cycle in Scots, he went on to teach creative writing at the University of Dundee's Duncan of Jordanstone. He died in 2010.

Andy Jackson was born in Salford in 1965, moving to Fife in 1992, later to work as Medical Librarian in the University of Dundee. He began writing poetry in earnest in 2002 and has been published in a variety of poetry magazines including *New Writing Scotland, Gutter* and *Magma*. He won the National Galleries of Scotland competition in 2008 and the inaugural Baker Prize in 2011. Andy's first collection *The Assassination Museum* was published in 2010 by Red Squirrel Press, for whom he subsequently compiled and edited *Split Screen: poems inspired by film & television*. He is working on a second full collection and is soon to revive the *Seagate* poetry anthology for the 21st Century.

Kathleen Jamie is a poet, author, and educator. Born in Renfrewshire in 1962, she studied philosophy at Edinburgh University where her first poems were published in *Black Spiders* (1982), winning an Eric Gregory Award and a Scottish Arts Council Book Award. She has gone on to publish eleven further works, including poetry collections, books of essays, and a collaboration with poet Andrew Greig. Consistently shortlisted for poetry awards, her wins include the Forward Poetry Prize and the Scottish Book of the Year Award. She has held several writer-in-residence posts, including Creative Writing Fellow at the University of Dundee, 1991-1993.

Arthur Johnston was a physician and poet. Born in Aberdeenshire circa 1579, he is thought to have studied at the University of Aberdeen before receiving an M.D. at Padua, Italy, in 1610. He spent a period of time teaching and practicing in Paris before returning to Aberdeen after the death of King James VI/I. Johnston left more than ten works, all composed in Latin, including an anthology of contemporary Latin verse by Scottish poets. His volume *Cantici Salomonis paraphrasis poetica*, published the year of Charles I's Scottish coronation and dedicated to the new sovereign, brought him contemporary fame.

William Johnston's 'To Joseph Lee' was taken from *Sword & Pen*.

Dorothy Lawrenson is an artist, poet, and graphic designer from Dundee, currently living in Edinburgh. Her poems have been published in *Markings* and the *Edinburgh Review*, and her pamphlets *Under the Threshold* (2006) and *Upon a good high hill (2011), which include her own photographs and sketches,* were shortlisted for Callum Macdonald Memorial Awards.

Edward Lear was a poet, author, artist, and illustrator. He is renowned primarily for his nonsense poetry. Born in 1812 in London, he was the twentieth of twenty-one children and raised by his sister due to his parents' bankruptcy. He began earning money as an illustrator at the age of 15. He suffered throughout his life from general ill health, including asthma, epilepsy, and depression. His *Book of Nonsense* (1846), a volume exclusively of limericks, popularised the form and secured his reputation, though his most famous piece of nonsense remains *The Owl and the Pussycat* (1871).

Joseph Lee was a journalist, artist, cartoonist, and poet. Born in Dundee in 1876, he wrote for, produced, and edited several local periodicals, including *The Piper O' Dundee* and *The City Echo*. Publishing his poetry regularly in the local newspaper *The People's Journal*, his first collection, *Tales O' Our Town*, was published in 1910. His play *Fra Lippo Lippi* was produced and performed by students of the Dundee Technical College and School of Art, now Abertay University. At the outbreak of WWI he joined the 4th Battalion of the Black Watch, aged 40, and chronicled in poetry and prose life in the trenches and his experiences as a POW. He returned to Dundee in 1944 and died in 1949. He is frequently described as 'Scotland's Forgotten War Poet'. His papers are now held in the Archives at the University of Dundee.

L.A. Lefevre was a poet and philanthropist. Born in Ontario, Canada, in 1853, she was an active member of the Canadian Authors' Association, a founder of the Vancouver Art Gallery, and also organised Vancouver's first Imperial Order of Daughters of the Empire (IODE) chapter on Edward VII's coronation. While living in Vancouver with her husband, her home – *Langaravine* – also functioned as a social centre for over fifty years. Her first poetry collection, *The Lion's Gate*, published in 1895, was republished in 1936 to celebrate Vancouver's jubilee. She died in Vancouver in 1938.

Robert Leighton was born in Dundee in 1822 and worked in the family shipping business. In 1849 he wrote for a Dundee pamphlet several poems and songs of which *Jenny Marshall's Candy O* proved instantly popular. In 1855 *Poems by Robin* was published and in 1866 *Poems by Robert Leighton*. Leighton was famous for reciting one of his early compositions *The Laddie's Lamentation on the Loss O' his Whittle* and *The Centenary of Robert Burns* which he recited at the Ayr gathering in 1859. Leighton's complete works are included in the two volumes *Reuben and other Poems* (1875) and *Records and other Poems* (1880). He died in Liverpool in 1869.

Pippa Little was born in Africa, raised in St. Andrews, and now lives in Northumberland. She has been the recipient of an Eric Gregory Award, The Andrew Waterhouse Prize, The Biscuit International Poetry Prize, and The Norman MacCaig Centenary Poetry Prize. Her publications include *The Spar Box* (2006), which was a Poetry Book Society Pamphlet Choice, *Foray* (2009), and *The Snow Globe* (2011). *Overwintering*, her latest, was published by Oxford Poets/ Carcanet in 2012.

Anna MacDonald was a prolific writer of poems in dialect during the 1980s and 1990s. Her poem 'Busters' is taken from the pamphlet *Dundee Tenement Talk* (1998).

Carl MacDougall is a writer, television presenter, radio broadcaster, editor, and reviewer. Born in Glasgow and raised throughout Central Scotland, he founded and edited *Words* magazine, where extracts from Alasdair Gray's *Lanark* and stories by James Kelman and Agnes Owens first appeared. He has written three prize-winning novels – *Stone Over Water, The Lights Below,* and *The Casanova Papers* – stage adaptations of *The Good Soldier Schweik* and Molière's *Don Juan*, and edited several books including the classic Scottish short story anthology *The Devil and the Giro*. With several published poems to his name, he is also the author of *Painting the Forth Bridge: A Search for Scottish Identity*. Billy Connolly has called him 'a hero of mine, a great storyteller'.

Lorraine McCann was born in Dundee in 1964. Graduating with an English degree from the University of Dundee, she works as a freelance writer and actor. She wrote the dramas *A Rose for Chopin* (2002) and *The Trading Game* (2004) for BBC Radio 4 and several successful one-act comedies for fringe theatre. Her debut novel, *Centrepiece*, was shortlisted for the inaugural Dundee Book Prize (1999) and subsequently published. In 2008, she won first prize in the prestigious Brian Moore Short Story Competition.

Ellie McDonald writes: 'The long-established tradition of autobiographical notes may satisfy the curious but answers no relevant questions'.

William McGonagall was born in Edinburgh in 1825, moving to his 'home city' of Dundee to apprentice as a handloom weaver. At the age of 52, an epiphany prompted him to devote the rest of his life to poetry. Though commonly cited as one of the worst poets in the English language, his work continues to enjoy considerable popularity. Gaining notoriety in his lifetime for his poetry readings, including regular appearances at a local circus during which he was pelted with fruit and veg, he can be considered an early performance artist. Seven collections of his work were circulated in his lifetime, including *Poetic Gems, More Poetic Gems, Still More Poetic Gems*, and *Yet More Poetic Gems*. There are several tributes to McGonagall throughout Dundee, including memorials, inscriptions, and place-names in his honour. He continues to be referenced in works of popular culture, including the *Harry Potter* series. He died in Edinburgh in 1902.

Hugh McMillan is a poet and short story writer. Born in 1955, he lives in Penpont and teaches History at Dumfries Academy. His pamphlet 'Postcards from the Hedge' was a winner of the Callum Macdonald Prize (2009). He is also a winner of the Smith Doorstep Poetry Prize, the Cardiff International Poetry Competition, the Scottish National Open Poetry Prize, and has been the recipient of several Scottish Arts Council Bursaries. He has four collections of poetry, including *Aphrodite's Anorak* (1996) and *The Lost Garden* (2010).

Michael Marra was a songwriter and musician. Born in Dundee in 1952, he was predominantly known as a solo performer though he worked extensively in theatre, radio, and television. He opened for such diverse performers as Van Morrison, The Proclaimers, Loudon Wainwright III, Barbara Dickson, and Deacon Blue. He devised the show 'In Flagrant Delicht' in collaboration with poet and playwright Liz Lochhead. His operetta 'If The Moon Can Be Believed' was performed at the Dundee Rep theatre to sell-out audiences. He wrote the popular song 'Hamish the Goalie' about ex-Dundee United goalkeeper Hamish McAlpine. In 2007 Michael was awarded an Honorary Doctorate from the University of Dundee in recognition of his contribution to the cultural profile of his home town. Michael died in 2012, mourned not just by the people of Dundee but all of Scotland.

Henry Marsh was born in Broughty Ferry, Dundee, in 1944 and now lives in Midlothian. He spent his working life teaching English and Philosophy. His PhD thesis was a study of the modes of imagination. Having written poetry since 2000, he has had four poetry collections published, including *A First Sighting* (2005) and *The Hammer and the Fire* (2011). He has also worked in collaboration with artist Kym Needle to produce two collections of poems and paintings on Australia.

George Maxwell's 'Prospect from Balgay' is taken from *Tay Pearls: A book of original poetry by the people of Dundee 1879-1905*, edited by Catherine Cairnie and published in 1993 by Urban Print.

Gordon Meade is a poet and creative writing workshop facilitator. He has published six full-length poetry collections, including *The Familiar* (2011) and *The Cleaner Fish* (2006). In 1993-1995 he was the Creative Writing Fellow at the Duncan of Jordanstone College of Art and Writer in Residence for Dundee District Libraries. Since 2000, Gordon has run creative writing workshops for vulnerable young people in a variety of settings and has edited three anthologies of young people's poetry. He lives with his family in the East Neuk of Fife.

David Millar's *The Tay: A Poem* was published in 1850. Written and published in Perth, the poem was printed in a single book-length volume and consists of five cantos. In the poem's Preface, Millar addresses his subscribers, suggesting it to be a small pre-subscribed publication for local residents. He writes that 'it is not very likely that his Volume will find its way far beyond the locality it treats of'.

William Montgomerie was born in Glasgow in 1904. Graduating from the University of Glasgow, he spent a period teaching in Dundee before collecting Scottish folksongs and ballads for the University of Edinburgh's School of Scottish Studies. With his wife, Norah Montgomerie, he edited four collections of folklore, verse, and children's rhymes. His publications include *The Well at the World's End* (1956) and *The Hogarth Book of Scottish Nursery Rhymes* (1964). He died in 1994.

Carolina Nairne was a songwriter and song collector. She was born in the Auld Hoose of Gask, Perthshire, in 1776. Her father, Lawrence Oliphant, was one of the foremost supporters of the Jacobite cause. Following the example set by Robert Burns in the *Scots Musical Museum*, Lady Nairne collected national airs set to appropriate words and published them alongside a large number of original songs. Her own compositions, such as 'Will Ye No' Come Back Again?', are now considered Scottish folk classics. She died at Gask in 1845.

Alexander Nicol was born in 1739, the son of a packman. Though attending school for only one year, he educated himself while following his father's trade and became teacher of English at Abernyte, Perthshire. His two poetry publications were *Nature without Art* (1739) and *Nature's Progress in Poetry* (1739). These volumes were reprinted in one volume in 1766, under the title *Poems on Several Subjects, both comical and serious*. He died in 1766.

Sean O'Brien is a multi-award-winning poet, critic, playwright, and author. Born in London in 1952, he is one of only two poets to have won both the T. S. Eliot Prize and the Forward Poetry Prize for the same collection – *The Drowned Book* (2007). He has written six collections of poetry and authored a range of other works, including short story collections, essays, plays, a novel, and a verse translation of Dante's *Inferno* (2006). He was co-founder of the literary magazine *The Printer's Devil* and regularly contributes to newspapers and magazines. He is Vice-President of the Poetry Society and Professor of Creative Writing at Newcastle University.

Honor Patching is a poet and author. Born in Brighton, Sussex, she moved to the East Neuk of Fife in 1984. Beginning to write in earnest while in Scotland, her prose and poetry has since been published by Chapman, *London Magazine*, Polygon, *Outposts*, and *Panurge*.

Don Paterson was born in Dundee in 1963. He is a multi-award-winning poet, writer, and musician. Along with his collections of poetry, including *God's Gift to Women* (1997), he has written plays, radio dramas, books of aphorisms, and he has edited several poetry anthologies. He currently teaches Creative Writing in the School of English, St Andrews University. He is an accomplished jazz guitarist.

David Phillips was a journalist and author based in Dundee. Working as a painter on prefabs in Dundee after WWII, he first contributed short articles and photographs about hillwalking to various newspapers and magazines before turning to poetry. His first collection, *The Lichty Nichts and other writings in the Dundee Dialect*, appeared in 1969, and his poems have appeared in such places as the *Evening Telegraph*, the *Weekly Scotsman*, and been broadcast on the BBC's Home Service and Overseas Service. His autobiography, *I Never Fell into a Midden*, was published in 1978. His other publications include *Oor Dundee* (1977), *Pictorial Dundee* (1980), and *The Hungry Thirties: Dundee Between the Wars* (1981). He died in 1987.

William J Rae was born in London to Scottish parents. After service during the Second World War he attended the University of Aberdeen, spending subsequent years teaching and lecturing in the Dundee area. Before retirement he was a Senior Lecturer in Academic Studies at Dundee College. His poetry and his short stories and fables appear regularly in various magazines and literary publications.

Lydia Robb is twice winner of the Hugh MacDiarmid Trophy and has won the McLellan Silver Tassie in the Scots Language Competition and the Scottish Book Trust Poetry Competition. She works for the Broughty Ferry Environmental Trust running poetry workshops for adults and children. She currently lives in a cottage in the Angus countryside. Her first full-length poetry collection, *Last Tango with Magritte*, was published in 2001.

Gary Robertson is a poet and author from Dundee, self-styled as the 'Dundee Street Poet'. Focusing on the culture and experience of youth in the city, he is the author of *Gangs of Dundee*, a historical account of post-war gang culture; *What's it All About Ralphie?*, a biography of ex-Dundee United footballer Ralph Milne; and *Pure Dundee*, his first poetry collection. His work was used in the documentary *Young Anes*, which depicted the life of a struggling young Dundonian mother and was shortlisted for an Edinburgh International Film Festival award. With Mark Thomson he was one half of *Tribal Tongues*, a poetry-performing duo based in Dundee, and is also singer and piper with Dundee's 'Oary Rock' band *The Cundeez*.

The Roper Bard, George Watson, worked in the rope trade in Dundee from an early age. He continued his education through night classes and gained renown as the popular poet 'The Roper Bard'. He died in Dundee, 1914, aged 68. Handwritten volumes of his poetry dating from 1885 to 1904 are held by Dundee City Libraries – presented by his son, George Watson, Canada, in 1952. Pages can be seen on Scotland's online educational resource, SCRAN.

Elliot Rudie was born in Dundee in 1939. After completing a Diploma in Drawing and Painting from the Duncan and Jordanstone College of Art in 1960, he pursued a career as an artist between Scotland and France. In Paris he spent time at the 'Beat Hotel' – an establishment central to the Beat poetry movement – and has since been involved in a documentary film on the hotel and its famous clientele. Returning from Paris after the hotel's closure in 1963, he worked in Scotland as a Principal Teacher of Art for thirty years. His painting and poetry has appeared throughout the UK.

J.B. Salmond was born in Arbroath in 1891, and was educated there and at St Andrews University. He moved to London to become a journalist and enlisted in a Territorial Army unit initially before being commissioned in the 7th Black Watch, where he saw heavy fighting on the Western Front at Arras and the Somme. Most of his war poetry was written in the vernacular and exhibits the tone and voice of the ordinary soldier. In 1918, Salmond became editor of the *Scots Magazine* in Dundee and wrote his vernacular verse under the nom-de-plume of 'Wayfarer'. His poetry was collected in *Old Stalker and Other Poems* and published in 1936.

Andrew Murray Scott, born in 1955, was a leading force behind Dundee-based literary magazines AMF/Logos in the 1970s and Riverrun 2000-2002. His fifteen book titles include four novels – *Tumulus* (winner of the inaugural Dundee Book Prize), *Estuary Blue, The Mushroom Club, The Big J* – and a poetry collection, *Dancing Underwater.* His two-volume cultural guide, *Dundee's Literary Lives,* is available from Abertay Historical Society and his influential biography *Alexander Trocchi: The Making of the Monster* was reprinted in 2012 by Kennedy & Boyd. He is presently completing a fifth novel, *Bruised Souls,* partly set in Dundee in 1983.

Tom Scott was a poet, editor, and author. Born in Glasgow in 1918, he served in the Royal Army in Britain and Nigeria during World War II. After service he earned a PhD in English Literature from Edinburgh University. His first poems were published in 1941 and he received an Atlantic Award for Literature in 1950. His publications include *Seeven Poems o Maister Francis Villon: Made Oure intil Scots* (1953) and *At the Shrine o the Unkent Sodger: A Poem for Recitation* (1968). He died in 1995.

Walter Scott was a historical novelist, poet, and playwright. Born in Edinburgh in 1771, he studied at the University of Edinburgh and was apprenticed to become a Writer to the Signet. He was the first author to have an internationally successful career in his lifetime. The Scott Monument was built on Edinburgh's Princes Street in his honour. Dundee features fairly regularly in his work, including his novel *Waverley* (1818) and his poem and song *Bonnie Dundee* (1828).

Norval Scrimgeour was a local journalist and poet, working in the 1890s. His poetry was collected in *City Songs*, published by Wm Kidd in 1893 after appearing in a plethora of magazines and newspapers.

Syd Scroggie was a writer, poet, and hillwalker. Born to Scottish parents in Canada in 1919, he was brought to Dundee as a baby, his father dying of wounds received during WWI. He attended John Watson's, Edinburgh, and Harris Academy, Dundee, before joining publishers D. C. Thomson where he was employed as a sub-editor. During the final months of WWII, while serving as an officer in Italy, Syd stepped on an anti-personnel mine and lost his right leg and the use of both eyes. He returned from service to learn Braille at St Dunstan's, London, and study at New College, Oxford. Settling again in Dundee, he worked for NCR and continued to pursue his love of hillwalking, making more than 600 blind climbs. In 1964 he appeared on the popular television show *This Is Your Life*. He taught himself Greek and became a published author and poet, his works including *The Cairngorms: Scene and Unseen* (1989) and his collected poems *Give Me the Hills* (1978). He received an honorary doctorate from the University of Dundee in 2001. He died in 2006.

Brenda Shaw was born in Maine and studied at Boston University, receiving a doctorate in biological sciences. Moving to Dundee with her husband, she worked as a researcher, lecturer, and senior lecturer at the University of Dundee's Medical School. Besides her numerous scientific writings, her short stories, non-fiction, and poetry has appeared in various anthologies and publications on both sides of the Atlantic. She edited an anthology of Dundee poetry, *Seagate II* (1984), and saw her own first collection, *The Cold Winds of Summer*, published by Dundee publishers Blind Serpent in 1987 and prefaced by Douglas Dunn. Both books received grants from the Scottish Arts Council. Between 1987 and 2003 she returned to the States, settling in Oregon to pursue her writing career. In 2003 she returned to her permanent home in Dundee.

Susan Sim's 'Home Town' appeared in Dundee University's *Gallimaufry* magazine in 1985.

Harry Smart is a writer, poet, artist and photographer. Born in Yorkshire in 1956, he gained a PhD from the University of Aberdeen and now lives in Montrose. He has had three poetry collections published – *Shoah* (1993), *Pierrot* (1994), and *Fool's Pardon* (1995) – and a novel, *Zaire* (1997). He recently graduated with a Fine Art degree from Duncan of Jordanstone, University of Dundee.

John Smith's 'Davit Dick, Dundee Carrier' is taken from *Poems & Lyrics* (1888), published by Miller & Gall of Perth. The publication refers to the author as John Smith of Alyth (otherwise known as 'Auld C').

Stan Smith was born in Warrington, Lancashire, and took his undergraduate and doctoral degrees at Jesus College, Cambridge. After a year lecturing at Aberdeen University he was one of two people appointed in 1968 to set up the new department of English at Dundee University, after its separation from St Andrews. He taught there for thirty years, as Lecturer, Senior Lecturer, and Reader, being appointed to the established Chair in 1989. In 1999 he accepted an invitation to take up a Research Chair in English at Nottingham Trent University, where he is now an emeritus professor. He has written and edited many books on modern and contemporary literature, the most recent of which is *Poetry and Displacement* (2007). He is general editor of Longman Critical Readers, Longman Studies in Twentieth-Century Literature, and Irish Writers in their Time. A first collection of poems, *Family Fortunes*, was published by Shoestring Press in 2008.

Lewis Spence was a folklorist, poet, and occult scholar. Born in 1874 in Broughty Ferry, Dundee, he graduated from the University of Edinburgh to pursue a career in journalism. An interest in anthropology and world mythology claimed his attention and he published over thirty books on the subject, including *The Myths of Mexico and Peru* (1914), *The History of Atlantis* (1927), and *The Magic Arts in Celtic Britain* (1949). He was the founder of the Scottish National Movement, which later merged to form the Scottish National Party. His *Collected Poems* were published in 1953. He died in Edinburgh in 1955.

Kenneth C Steven was born in Glasgow in 1968 and raised in Highland Perthshire. He has studied and taught in Norway and translated from both Norwegian and Sami. A widely published poet, novelist, and children's writer, his full-length poetry collections include *Evensong* (2011) and *Island: Collected Poems* (2009). His translation of Lars Saaybe Christensen's *Half Brother* was a finalist for the 2004 Independent Foreign Fiction Prize.

Anne Stevenson is an American poet and writer who has lived in Britain for over 40 years. She has published more than a dozen volumes of poetry, including *Astonishment* (2012) and *Granny Scarecrow* (2000). She was Writer in Residence at the University of Dundee from 1973 to 1975 and founded the writing group which produced the first Dundee anthology *Seagate*. In 2007 she received the Lannan Award for a Lifetime's Achievement in Poetry and the Poetry Foundation of America's Neglected Masters Award.

Jim Stewart was born in Dundee in 1952. He took an MA in English at the University of Dundee in 1984; and the PhD at Edinburgh in 1990. A Modernist scholar, his specialism is Virginia Woolf: he is co-editing Woolf's first novel *The Voyage Out* for the Cambridge University Press Edition. He has taught English at Dundee University since 1988, and also teaches Creative Writing there with the novelist Kirsty Gunn. He has published poetry in various national and international outlets; and is writing the libretto for an opera on Flora Macdonald, composed by Graham Robb.

David Strachan was born in Edinburgh. After graduating from St Andrews University with an Honours degree in English Literature and completing a Fulbright scholarship in Schenectady in American Studies, he saw national service in the R.A.F and colonial service in Kenya. Upon returning to Scotland he taught at secondary schools in Glasgow and Dundee. His short fiction and poetry has been published and broadcast in Kenya and the UK, including *The Scotsman, New Writing Scotland, Chapman* and *Riverrun*, and he is a former Winner of The MacAllan Short Story Competition. His play *Turning Point* was produced in Nairobi and his *Dog in the Bath* was produced in Edinburgh.

F.W. Swan's *The Worthies O' Dundee*, a long work from which an extract is taken and reproduced here, was published in 1892.

Judith Taylor was born in Perthshire and currently lives in Aberdeen. She studied English and Mediaeval History at the University of St Andrews. A librarian by profession, she is also a member of the editorial team at *Pushing Out the Boat* magazine. Her first chapbook collection, *Earthlight*, was published in 2006 and her second, *Local Colour*, in 2010.

James Hall Thomson was born in Dundee in 1937, worked from 1955 as cartoonist/caricaturist for DC Thomson, Scottish Daily Mail, Melody Maker and many other publications. Parallel to this contributed a variety of poetry to numerous magazines including *Lallans*. Won the Willie Graham Award for best poem in *Lallans* in 1994. Designed covers for Court Poetry Press booklets and others. Chairman of Dundee University Writers Group for sixteen years up to 2004 and along with Margaret Gillies Brown attended Saggar Poets for twenty-five years. Continues to edit and revise existing work.

Mark Thomson is a poet, performer, and creative writing teacher. Born and raised in Dundee in the 1980s, he worked for a decade as a labourer before pursuing a full-time writing career. He works across Scotland with community groups and statutory and voluntary organisations in places as diverse as prisons, classrooms, and football stadiums, and speaks regularly at national cultural, literacy, and voluntary sector conferences. With Gary Robertson he was one half of *Tribal Tongues*, a poetry performing duo based in Dundee. His collection *Bard Fae The Building Site* was published in 2007.

George Walter Thornbury was born in London in 1828. A journalist by profession, he also wrote poetry, fiction, art criticism, and popular historical and topographical sketches. Beginning his career with contributions to *Bristol Journal*, and writing mainly for the *Athenaeum* and Charles Dickens's periodicals *Household Words* and *All the Year Round*, his publications include *Every Man His Own Trumpeter* (1858), *Old and New London* (1873-4), and *Historical and Legendary Ballads and Songs* (1875). He died at Camberwell House Asylum from 'overwork' in 1876.

Val Warner studied Modern History at Oxford and has worked as a teacher, freelance copy-editor, and freelance writer. She held the post of Writer in Residence at the University of Dundee, 1979-1981. She has published translations of Tristan Corbiere, *The Centenary Corbiere*, and edited *The Collected Poems & Prose of Charlotte Mew*. Her poetry, for which she has received a Gregory Award, has appeared in several full-length collections including *Under the Penthouse* (1973) and *Before Lunch* (1986).

George T. Watt was born in Clydebank, Dunbartonshire. Raised in Edinburgh, he began his working life on Islay and on various farms in the north east of Scotland before settling permanently in Dundee. Graduating from the University of Dundee in 2006 with First Class Honours in Literature, he writes in both Scots and English. George has a pamphlet published by Perjink, Edinburgh, entitled *Abune the Toun*, which is entirely in Scots.

Richard Watt is a journalist, reviewer, translator, musician, and poet. Born in Tayside, he studied English and Philosophy at university, tutored by poet Colette Bryce. He won the Dundee Poetry Prize in 2004. His latest poetry collection, *The Golem*, was published in 2012. He has translated a sheaf of German submarine poetry for the Black Watch Association. He is currently working on a novel: a penny-dreadful titled *Grotesques*.

John Wedderburn along with his brothers James and Robert, was a Reformist theologian. Born in 1505, he had been declared a heretic in 1539. The collection of poems *The Buik of Gude and Godlie Ballates* (sometimes known as the *Dundee Psalms*) was published in the late 1540s, and was intended to be a prayer book, but the verses were largely represented as profane ballads, appearing in vernacular Scots for the first time. After returning to Dundee from exile in 1546, he was forced to flee to England where he died in 1556.

Dawn Wood was born in 1963 in County Tyrone, Northern Ireland. She trained as a microbiologist at Queen's University, Belfast, before moving to Dundee in 1986. She now works as a science lecturer at the University of Abertay, Dundee, and as a painter. She completed her doctorate in 2008 on the husbandry of nature as poetry and as science. Her poetry collections include *Quarry, Connoisseur* and *Hermes With Gift*.

Douglas Young was a poet, scholar, and translator. Born in Tayport, he studied at St Andrews and Oxford universities and taught at Aberdeen and Dundee. A leading member of the emergent Scottish National Party, he was imprisoned in 1942 for refusing conscription (where he completed his first book of poems, *Auntran Blads*). He was renowned for his translations into Scots and earned an international reputation as a scholar of Greek, teaching classics in North America from the 1960s until his death.

ACKNOWLEDGEMENTS

Colette Bryce: 'Self-Portrait in the Dark (with Cigarette)' from *Self-Portrait in the Dark,* by Colette Bryce (Picador, 2008). Reprinted by permission of Macmillan Publishers Ltd.

John Burnside: 'Dundee' from *The Myth of the Twin*, by John Burnside (Jonathan Cape, 1994) Reprinted by permission of The Random House Group Ltd. 'Children Sledding in the Dark, Magdalen Green' from *A Normal Skin,* by John Burnside (Jonathan Cape, 1997) Reprinted by permission of The Random House Group Ltd. 'The Unprovable Fact: A Tayside Inventory' from *The Asylum Dance,* by John Burnside (Jonathan Cape, 2000) Reprinted by permission of The Random House Group Ltd.

Robert Crawford: 'Mary Shelley on Broughty Ferry Beach' from *Talkies,* by Robert Crawford (Chatto and Windus, 1992) Reprinted by permission of The Random House Group Ltd. 'The Catalogue of Ships' from *Talkies,* by Robert Crawford (Chatto and Windus, 1992) Reprinted by permission of The Random House Group Ltd.

Douglas Dunn: 'Broughty Ferry' from *New Selected Poems,* by Douglas Dunn (Faber and Faber, 2003) Reprinted by permission of Faber and Faber Ltd. 'Leaving Dundee' from *New Selected Poems,* by Douglas Dunn (Faber and Faber, 2003) Reprinted by permission of Faber and Faber Ltd. 'Tay Bridge' from *New Selected Poems,* by Douglas Dunn (Faber and Faber, 2003) Reprinted by permission of Faber and Faber Ltd.

G.F. Dutton: G F Dutton: 'Call', 'Craigie Park, 'Grown Up' and 'Occasions' from *The Bare Abundance: Poems 1970-2001*, by G F Dutton (Bloodaxe Books, 2002) Reprinted by permission of Bloodaxe Books Ltd.

Matthew Fitt: 'Discovery' from *Kate O'Shanter's Tale,* by Matthew Fitt (Luath Press, 2003) Reprinted by permission of Luath Press Ltd. 'Liz McColgan' from *Kate O'Shanter's Tale,* by Matthew Fitt (Luath Press, 2003) Reprinted by permission of Luath Press Ltd.

Bashabi Fraser: 'From the Ganga to the Tay: Dundee Connection' from *From the Ganga to the Tay*, by Bashabi Fraser (Luath Press, 2009) Reprinted by permission of Luath Press Ltd.

John Glenday: 'Etching of a Line of Trees' from *Grain*, by John Glenday (Picador, 2009) Reprinted by permission of Macmillan Publishers Ltd. 'Etching of a Line of Trees' from *Grain*, by John Glenday (Picador, 2009) Reprinted by permission of Macmillan Publishers Ltd.

W.N. Herbert: 'Ode to the New Old Tay Bridge' from *Bad Shaman Blues*, by W.N. Herbert (Bloodaxe Books, 2006) Reprinted by permission of Bloodaxe Books Ltd. '2nd Doldrum' from *Forked Tongue*, by W.N. Herbert (Bloodaxe Books, 1994) Reprinted by permission of Bloodaxe Books Ltd. 'Port Selda' from *The Laurelude*, by W.N. Herbert (Bloodaxe Books, 1998) Reprinted by permission of Bloodaxe Books Ltd. 'The Great Camperdown Breakout' from *The Big Bumper Book of Troy*, by W.N. Herbert (Bloodaxe Books, 2002) Reprinted by permission of Bloodaxe Books Ltd. 'A Lament for Billy Mackenzie' from *The Big Bumper Book of Troy*, by W.N. Herbert (Bloodaxe Books, 2002) Reprinted by permission of Bloodaxe Books Ltd.

Kathleen Jamie: 'The Tay Moses' from *Jizzen*, by Kathleen Jamie (Picador, 1999) Reprinted by permission of Macmillan Publishers Ltd.

Henry Marsh: 'Dundee 1651' from *A First Sighting*, by Henry Marsh (Maclean Dubois, 2005) Reprinted by permission of Birlinn Ltd.

William McGonagall: 'Burial of the Rev. George Gilfillan' from *Collected Poems*, by William McGonagall (Birlinn, 2006) Reprinted by permission of Birlinn Ltd. 'The Famous Tay Whale' from *Collected Poems*, by William McGonagall (Birlinn, 2006) Reprinted by permission of Birlinn Ltd. 'The Tay Bridge Disaster' from *Collected Poems*, by William McGonagall (Birlinn, 2006) Reprinted by permission of Birlinn Ltd.

Gordon Meade: 'Mist' from *The Cleaner Fish*, by Gordon Meade (Arrowhead Press, 2006) Reprinted by permission of Arrowhead Press Ltd. 'The Estuary' from *The Familiar*, by Gordon Meade (Arrowhead Press, 2011) Reprinted by permission of Arrowhead Press Ltd.

Sean O'Brien: 'At the Wellgate' from *Cousin Coat*, by Sean O'Brien (Picador, 2002) Reprinted by permission of Macmillan Publishers Ltd. 'Dundee Heatwave' from *Cousin Coat*, by Sean O'Brien (Picador, 2002) Reprinted by permission of Macmillan Publishers Ltd.

Don Paterson: '00:00: Law Tunnel' from *God's Gift to Women*, by Don Paterson (Faber and Faber, 2005) Reprinted by permission of Faber and Faber Ltd. '11:00: Baldovan' from *God's Gift to Women*, by Don Paterson (Faber and Faber, 2005) Reprinted by permission of Faber and Faber Ltd. 'Addenda' from *God's Gift to Women*, by Don Paterson (Faber and Faber, 2005) Reprinted by permission of Faber and Faber Ltd.

Lydia Robb: 'Crossing the Tay Bridge' from *Last Tango with Magritte*, by Lydia Robb (Chapman Publishing, 2001) Reprinted by permission of Chapman Publishing. 'Dundee Day Tripper' from *Last Tango with Magritte*, by Lydia Robb (Chapman Publishing, 2001) Reprinted by permission of Chapman Publishing. 'National Poetry Day' from *Last Tango with Magritte*, by Lydia Robb (Chapman Publishing, 2001) Reprinted by permission of Chapman Publishing.

Gary Robertson: 'A Dihzeez Ca'd Dundonese' from *Pure Dundee*, by Gary Robertson (Luath Press, 2007) Reprinted by permission of Luath Press Ltd. 'Jimmy Reid's' from *Pure Dundee*, by Gary Robertson (Luath Press, 2007) Reprinted by permission of Luath Press Ltd. 'Thi La' Hill' from *Pure Dundee*, by Gary Robertson (Luath Press, 2007) Reprinted by permission of Luath Press Ltd.

Tom Scott: 'Dundee Hospital Ward' from *The Collected Shorter Poems*, by Tom Scott (Chapman Publishing, 1993) Reprinted by permission of Chapman Publishing.

Harry Smart: 'The Hookers of Dundee' from *A Fool's Pardon*, by Harry Smart (Faber and Faber, 1995) Reprinted by permission of Faber and Faber Ltd.

Anne Stevenson: 'The Bench' from *Poems 1955-2005*, by Anne Stevenson (Bloodaxe Books, 2005) Reprinted by permission of Bloodaxe Books Ltd. 'The Lighthouse' from *Poems 1955-2005*, by Anne Stevenson (Bloodaxe Books, 2005) Reprinted by permission of Bloodaxe Books Ltd. 'The Mudtower' from *Poems 1955-2005*, by Anne Stevenson (Bloodaxe Books, 2005) Reprinted by permission of Bloodaxe Books Ltd.

Mark Thomson: 'Thi Mither Tongue' from *Bard fae thi Buildin Site*, by Mark Thomson (Luath Press, 2007) Reprinted by permission of Luath Press Ltd.

Val Warner: 'Going Home' from *Before Lunch*, by Val Warner (Carcanet, 1986) Reprinted by permission of Carcanet Press Ltd. 'Drawing the Curtain' from *Before Lunch*, by Val Warner (Carcanet, 1986) Reprinted by permission of Carcanet Press Ltd. 'Warp' from *Before Lunch*, by Val Warner (Carcanet, 1986) Reprinted by permission of Carcanet Press Ltd.

Richard Watt: '45, Ark Road (Park Road)' from *The Golem*, by Richard Watt (Hold Fire Press, 2012) Reprinted by permission of Hold Fire Press. 'Dundonian U.X.O.' from *The Golem*, by Richard Watt (Hold Fire Press, 2012) Reprinted by permission of Hold Fire Press. 'Stobswell Set Radio Future' from *The Golem*, by Richard Watt (Hold Fire Press, 2012) Reprinted by permission of Hold Fire Press.